DISCOVER
FORTH

DISCOVER FORTH

Learning and Programming The FORTH Language

Thom Hogan

Osborne/McGrawHill
Berkeley, California

Illustrated by
Mary M. Milewski

Published by
Osborne/McGraw-Hill
630 Bancroft Way
Berkeley, California   94710
USA

For information on other Osborne books, translations and distributors outside of the U.S.A., please write Osborne/McGraw-Hill at the above address.

Discover FORTH: Learning and Programming
the FORTH Language

ISBN 0-931988-79-9

1 2 3 4 5 6 7 8 9 0 HCHC 89098765432

Text and cover design by Irene Imfeld

Okay, Dick, you got me into this — now get me out!

Contents

ACKNOWLEDGMENTS

The author would like to thank Eva Hogan and Dick Milewski for their technical and editorial assistance. The publisher wishes to express gratitude to Jim Flournoy for his technical review.

After finishing my first book, the *Osborne CP/M™ User Guide*[1], I expected to go back to completing one of the two other book projects I had started.

Instead, I accepted a job at *Info World*, where I met Dick Milewski. If each person has a lookalike somewhere on this planet, I suppose he must have a spiritual twin, too. Dick is my spiritual twin.

Within a few weeks of meeting Dick, I knew that his passion for the language FORTH would probably be passed on to me. I listened to Dick's explanation of FORTH's virtues. I watched as he glibly programmed small miracles (he called them "words") on the North Star computer in my office. I was hooked.

I soon found myself wandering through the aisles of bookstores looking for any book that would explain FORTH to me. There weren't any.

It was at about that time that Dick gave me a preliminary release of his latest programming project, "The Software Works FORTH." His manual helped, as did *Byte*'s special issue on the FORTH language.[2]

Then Dick, sneaky fellow that he is, suggested that one sure way of learning about FORTH would be to write a book about it. I was hooked again.

This book is an attempt to put what I've learned about FORTH into a coherent, organized introduction that others new to the language will appreciate.

Some of the material here is a tightly structured synthesis of material that appears in FORTH programming manuals, the FORTH Interest Group's[3] publications, and a few commented programs I have been able to obtain from serious FORTH programmers.

Many of the observations about the FORTH language come from my use of FORTH in a major software project. FORTH, however, is one

---

[1]Hogan, Thom. *Osborne CP/M™ User Guide*. Berkeley: Osborne/McGraw-Hill, 1981.
[2]August 1980 issue.
[3]Forth Interest Group, Box 1105, San Carlos, CA 94070, publishers of a journal entitled "FORTH Dimensions."

of those elusive languages that defy exact quantifying, so don't assume that what appears in this book is gospel — I'm sure that there are other advantages and disadvantages I have not pointed out, other possible shortcuts, and other conclusions to be drawn.

One last introductory comment before getting to the meat of the book: I have no particular love for the FORTH syntax, nor am I convinced that the definitive FORTH has yet appeared. It's up to you to create the FORTH you need by adding extensions and vocabularies.

I have tried to restrict myself to the syntax that both standard FORTH (FORTH-79) and FIG-FORTH use, but throughout this book I refer to logical extensions of the language as if they exist. I will try to point out any deviations from the 1979 FORTH standard as I use them.

Also, since I object to the "technobuzz" that permeates many FORTH definitions, you'll find a suggested alternative to the current FORTH syntax in Appendix D. FORTH program listings can be extremely difficult to read — especially if the program didn't use FORTH's flexible "commenting" facilities — and I think that some of my suggestions may help alleviate this problem.

T.H., Palo Alto, 1981

Chapter I

A Description of FORTH

"How forcible are right words!"
The Bible, Job VI, 25

One of the first things you'll hear anyone say about FORTH is that it is not a programming language, but a religion. FORTH programmers are often thought of as mystics, hunched over their video displays conjuring up micro mumbo-jumbo that somehow manages to make the machine behave. FORTH is a cryptic language, to be sure. It is also eye-catching. All the exclamation points that dot low-level FORTH programs suggest that the language drives programmers to exaggeration.

Another thing you'll hear about FORTH is that it is easy to write programs in it, but almost impossible to figure out what they do afterward. One story (most probably apocryphal) tells of a programmer who spent six months writing more than 150 screens of FORTH source code, only to discover that he couldn't figure out what the first ten screens were for. He tried the program with them — it worked. He took them out — it didn't work. He eventually put them back in, added a preface that said something like "change these ten screens at your own risk," and went on to his next project. Actually, most FORTH programmers are able to easily read their own code. It is generally more difficult to read someone else's FORTH program than it is to decipher your own, however.

If that weren't enough, you'll soon discover that the FORTH community has given "names," complete with correct pronunciations, to all of FORTH's symbolic notation. The logic in these assignments is not terribly consistent. You'll learn, for instance, that the FORTH word {!} is pronounced "store" while the FORTH word {R#} is pronounced "R-sharp." On the other hand, {UCASE} is pronounced "U-case."

This shouldn't scare you off. You might have heard horror stories about FORTH that kept you from closer inspection of the language. As you'll find in the rest of this book, FORTH can be accurately described using real English sentences, without magic spells, if one ignores the aberrations of those who have used FORTH for too long to be considered sane.

The Origin of FORTH

FORTH was invented around 1970 by Charles Moore. The inexactness of the date stems from the fact that Moore had contemplated and tried out bits and pieces of FORTH over a number of years before he actually fit it all together. Moore used an IBM 1130, one of the first fully interactive computers.

The name FORTH comes from Moore's conception of his invention as a fourth-generation computer language. Because the IBM 1130 accepted only five character identifiers, Moore shortened "fourth" to "FORTH."

In a speech at the FORTH Convention in San Francisco in 1979, Moore said that FORTH arose from work he had done at the Stanford Linear Accelerator Center and Mohasco. From a number of disparate pieces (an interpreter written in ALGOL, the "atom" concept of LISP, and early versions of FORTH coded in everything from FORTRAN to COBOL) FORTH eventually appeared as a complete programming language at the National Radio Astronomy Observatory (NRAO) in Kitt Peak, Arizona.

During the ensuing years, FORTH continued to evolve as Moore continued to expand on his initial programming for the NRAO. By 1973, Moore was so deluged by requests from astronomers to adapt his programming method to their systems that he and several others left NRAO to form FORTH, Incorporated. As Moore explained, "It is a market we would still be in today, except that there are so few new telescopes in the world, and you can't support a company on that market."

FORTH's development since 1973 centers around FORTH, Incorporated, and another informal group, the FORTH Interest Group (FIG). By 1979, Moore estimated, there were 1000 FORTH programmers, and that number was doubling every year. In addition, both Moore and the FIG think that FORTH is now available on almost every central-processing unit in existence.

The FORTH Qualities

FORTH has several attributes not commonly ascribed to computer languages.

First, FORTH is fast. The design of the language has been optimized for speed in many ways. Its rapidity is not surprising, considering its origins in controlling telescopes and other real-time devices.

Second, FORTH is small. It requires little computer support. Most FORTH systems require only 8K to 16K of RAM. The disadvantage that accompanies this conciseness is FORTH's lack of built-in floating-point arithmetic, string manipulators, and sophisticated disk input/output (I/O). Although these features can exist with FORTH, they are usually not provided with the basic system.

Last, FORTH is extensible. If you do not like the words (for now, consider these commands) available within a standard FORTH, you can create your own. You can take two words and combine them to create a new, third one. You can take that newly defined word, combine it with one or more other words, and create yet another function. In short, FORTH is a language of building blocks.

Programming in FORTH

The structure of FORTH is different from that of most languages. Thus, programming in FORTH is different than programming in, say, BASIC or COBOL.

FORTH defies description as either an interpreter or a compiler. The language contains elements of both. On the one hand, you can execute FORTH and immediately type words that FORTH recognizes and acts on as functions, as if it were an interpreter. On the other hand, you can type source code into an editor for reduction into machine language and later compilation and execution. With the interpreter shell of FORTH, you can also create new functions, which are compiled into a dictionary, using the language as an interpreter/ compiler combination.

To gain a full understanding of programming in FORTH, you should read this entire book. But for now, the following summary suffices to outline basic FORTH programming. Be careful. Some of this information is generalized. Refer to material supplied with your FORTH for specifics.

1. Load the FORTH Interpreter. Using your FORTH disk and the operating system of your computer, load and execute the FORTH interpreter just as you would any other machine-language program.

2. Create Program Blocks. Using the real-time capabilities of FORTH, begin to combine blocks of functions until, eventually, typing only a short series of words (or even just one) results in the action you desire. As you can see from the illustration, programming in FORTH is like creating a pyramid of small functions.

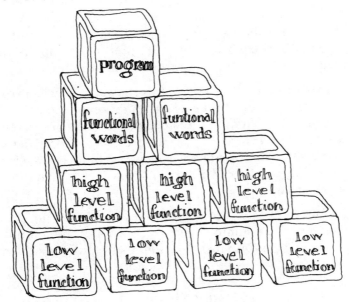

If you want a permanent program, you'll want to save your coding, so substitute the following steps for number two, above:

3. *Load the Editor.* Using the editor, create "screens" of FORTH source code, essentially, a formatted version of what you would type directly into FORTH to create new functions.

4. *Compile the Instructions.* In a standard FORTH system, the action of simply loading the screens of information into the computer using FORTH will compile the source code into an executable function or program. Some versions of FORTH (such as SL5 from The Stackworks) don't use the standard FORTH concept of "blocks" of information and thus require you to use a predefined word such as {FLOAD} to compile FORTH source code.

Note that the screens of information you load into FORTH can contain direct commands. Thus, you can accomplish what would normally be impossible in other languages, such as having the program invoke itself after compilation.

5. Use the Compiled Functions. The compiled code now functions exactly as if it were part of the overall FORTH interpreter. You may thus use your compiled code interactively or use it to build even bigger function blocks.

Again, you should be cautioned that the above descriptions are extreme generalizations. The terms "interpret" and "compile" are used in a very loose sense, as you will recognize soon enough.

If you've programmed a computer before, however, you'll have noticed that programming in FORTH is bizarrely different. Actually, there is more evidence to substantiate the conclusion that programming in FORTH is "kinky." Information is not necessarily stored in variables in a rational FORTH program. Instead, we encounter a concept called "stack" (basically an area of memory in which the last item stored is the first item retrieved).

Another quirk FORTH programmers live with is that almost all operations involving numbers use "reverse Polish notation," the technique of giving the numbers first and then stating what to do with them.

Using This Book

It is tempting to write a book about FORTH that tells you what you need to know about the language in reverse order of importance. After all, this is how you tell FORTH what to do. Fortunately, you've been saved the agony of reading from back to front, or as a programmer might say, "from the bottom up."

You must understand two primary components, the dictionary and the stack, to use FORTH. These appear in separate chapters immediately following this one.

The fourth chapter describes FORTH's arithmetic handling reverse Polish notation, and the integer-only attributes of FORTH.

Following these three general chapters are sections that deal with specific aspects of FORTH: the use of variables and constants, control structures, interface to devices, and memory manipulation. These chapters are the heart of this book and should serve as a computer-side reference.

The last portion of the book deals with handling FORTH's unique attributes and attempts to give you an idea of how to become an efficient FORTH programmer. Here I discuss how you can tailor FORTH to your general needs, develop working habits that suit the FORTH environment, and also tinker with such advanced things as the "return stack" and separate dictionaries.

Notational Conventions

To help you understand what you're reading, several conventions will remain consistent throughout this book. Every time a reference is made to a FORTH word in the text (as opposed to the examples), it will be enclosed in curly brackets ({EXAMPLEWORD}).

Another standard notation is that any special-function key will be set off between less-than and greater-than signs (a carriage return would be <ENTER> or <CR>, for example).

And finally, FORTH is used in its generic sense. Although FORTH is in the public domain, a trademark has been registered by FORTH, Incorporated. When something is stated about FORTH in this book, it specifically refers to FORTH-79 (the standardized FORTH) or FIG-FORTH (a public-domain version). To the extent that the vocabularies match, what is written here concerning FORTH applies to the products of FORTH, Inc., and other producers of the FORTH language as well.

You're now ready to discover FORTH.

Chapter 2

The
FORTH
Dictionary

"Suit the action to the word, the word to the action;
with this special observance, that you o'erstep not
the modest of nature."

Shakespeare, Hamlet, Act III, Scene II

This chapter will teach you about the basic structure of FORTH, which revolves around a concept called a "dictionary." You'll also learn about the components that go into the dictionary, FORTH "words."

Go Look It Up

In other languages, you tell the computer what to do by entering a series of commands or statements. Each command generally performs a single function. In almost every computer language, these commands are predetermined by the language designer, and you, the user, are restricted to those functions for which commands exist. You usually cannot delete, substitute, or change the functions.

FORTH is different. In FORTH, every function has a "word" associated with it. The word that is used to move a section of memory from one location to another, for instance, is {CMOVE}. For the time being, words will be treated much like commands in other languages; they each perform a function. Eventually that definition will be modified, but for now let it suffice.

Just like their English counterparts, FORTH words are defined in dictionaries. A FORTH dictionary is what is known as a "threaded" or "linked list" of variable-length items, each of which defines a word in the current vocabulary. The following is the general format for entries in a FORTH dictionary:

length of name ← # of characters
name ← dictionary entry
link pointer ← points to next entry
code pointer ← points to code for the word
parameters ← either a value (as for a variable) or a list of addresses

What this generalized format shows is that each dictionary entry keeps track of the length of the word, the letters that comprise the word itself, a linkage to another dictionary entry, an address to find the machine-language code associated with the word, and some parameters.

When FORTH needs to perform the actions you request by typing a valid word, it looks it up in the dictionary. What happens next depends upon whether the word you typed represents a constant, a variable, or a valid action. The differences are primarily in what information is stored in the "parameter field" of the dictionary entry.

─────────────What's in a Word─────────────

Most dictionary entries for FORTH words contain lists of memory addresses that point to other FORTH words. Only a few basic FORTH words actually contain machine language code and nothing else. The dictionary parameter field contains a list of addresses that represent other FORTH words that FORTH executes in sequence. The practical effect of such a list is to make FORTH "thread" its way back and forth through memory, executing words in a user-specified order. This is one of the attributes of FORTH that make it a "threaded language."

Here's an example. Suppose for a moment that you had three machine-language programs, all short, that performed the following three specific functions:

1. Retrieve a value stored somewhere in memory,

2. Subtract one from the value,

3. And see if the result is zero.

In FORTH, these three functions may be combined into one meta-function called {DTZ} (which stands for Decrement and Test for Zero). The word (meta-function) {DTZ} does not have any machine code located at the address associated with it, but instead has three addresses of the separate routines.

The flexibility that results from composing a word out of a series of other words is impressive.

Indeed, this is one of the primary attributes of FORTH. You can create new words by using already defined words. FORTH actually has the three routines listed above. They are called

1. {@}, which "fetches" a value from memory

2. {1-}, which subtracts one from the value retrieved

3. {0=}, which checks to see if the result was zero.

You could, therefore, create the function {DTZ} by simply telling FORTH to execute {@}, {1-}, and {0=}, in that order, every time it encounters {DTZ}.

Bargain Building Blocks

If you understood the description of what a word is, you should immediately grasp that FORTH is a "building-block" language. You use the vocabulary of words of standard FORTH to build larger metawords, which you can use to build meta-metawords, and so on.

The concept of programming in FORTH is building a pyramid. At the bottom of this pyramid you have all the possible FORTH words. Each successive layer of the pyramid is a distillation, a combination of the blocks of the previous one. Ultimately, the top of the pyramid is a single word that would command an entire sequence of events. This sequence of events is what is normally called a "program."

Admittedly, this is a dangerous oversimplification. Only small programming tasks are actually like pyramids. In reality, a large application program might end up looking like a number of pyramids, with some overlapping.

The pyramid image is a useful one, nonetheless, because it immediately forces you to recognize that a good FORTH program relies heavily on the "base" levels you construct.

Webster's, Oxford, Funk & Wagnall

As if the flexibility built into the structure described above were not enough, multiple dictionaries are possible in FORTH.

The primary advantage of multiple dictionaries is to allow you to switch the meaning of a word or set of words, depending upon the context in which you are using it. Words, in FORTH as in English, can have multiple meanings. The multiple dictionaries of FORTH allow you to fit meanings to the contexts in which they occur.

While multiple dictionaries aren't dealt with in detail here, as you become a better FORTH programmer you'll want to investigate this feature of the language more fully.

You haven't learned how to do anything in FORTH yet. What you have learned is how FORTH's structure and organization create a unique environment for programming.

Specifically, you now know the following basic principles:

• In FORTH, you invoke functions by typing words. In addition, many FORTH words invoke other FORTH words as part of their execution.

• FORTH words are defined in a dictionary, essentially in a linked list of words.

• A dictionary entry for a word consists of the length of the word name, the word name, the address of the previous word, the address of the machine code to be executed when the word is invoked, and some miscellaneous parameters (generally a list of addresses of other words to execute).

• A word is really just a list of instructions to perform.

• You combine words to create new ones.

• Programming in FORTH is the process of defining words.

• Simple FORTH programs are constructed like pyramids, each layer building on the previous one.

• Multiple dictionaries are possible and are used to change the "meaning" of a word, depending upon context.

Chapter 3

The Stack

" 'It's a poor sort of memory that only works backwards,' the Queen remarked."
Lewis Carroll, Through The Looking Glass

This chapter explains FORTH's unusual method of storing temporary information, called the "stack." You'll learn how FORTH allows you to manipulate a pile of information, albeit in a backward fashion.

FORTH and the Stack

Programs need to keep track of many details as they execute. This may mean simply keeping track of the characters you type, or keeping track of the results of calculations the programs need internally.

Traditionally, most computer languages use a concept called "variables" to store information a program needs. A variable is an area of the computer's memory reserved for storage and referenced by a name (the "variable name") you specify.

FORTH allows the use of variables, but, for the most part, an efficient FORTH program uses the stack for temporary storage of information.

Stacks are like a pile of plates. You always put additional plates on the top of the pile, and if you must take a plate off the pile, you take it off the top.

A FORTH stack is a pile of information. You add information to the top of the pile, one piece at a time. When it comes time to get information from the pile, you take it off the top, one element at a time.

This concept is sometimes referred to as a LIFO process (the acronym stands for Last In, First Out).

Why Use a Stack

Since FORTH allows variables, what advantage might there be in using the stack for storing temporary information? There are a number of possible answers to this question.

1. Speed. The stack offers two speed advantages. The first comes when you are using FORTH in the interpretive mode, and the second has to do with the inherent design of FORTH.

When acting as an interpreter, FORTH must figure out the location of variables by looking them up. Upon completion of this operation, a second step is moving the address of the located variable. Using the stack in most instances is a single-step process — one step to put something on, one step to take something off.

The inherent design of FORTH also plays a part in speed. Many of the words in the standard FORTH vocabulary expect to deal with numbers on the stack. Use of variables, although possible, often means that the programmer generates extra, unnecessary code.

Also, just because you retrieve the value stored in a variable doesn't mean that any new calculated value automatically will be stored in its place, as with most languages. The extra time that might result in trying to debug code that fails to update a variable correctly can also be considered a detriment to overall programming speed.

2. Convenience. Sometimes information is of a transient nature, and it is not worth going through the process of giving it a name and permanently storing it in memory. For example, suppose that your program needs to know which of three possible choices you want executed. The program will use the character you type to select which selection of code to run. But after that, the program will never use that character again.

If you put the character on the stack instead of storing it in a variable, it remains immediately accessible and is subsequently discarded after use.

3. *Sequential processing*. The stack is a "poor man's array." Sometimes several pieces of information need to be processed in sequence. You might have noted that the FORTH stack stores information in reverse sequential order.

To give you a simplified example, suppose that you type the numbers 1 through 10 and that each has been stored on the stack as you typed it. If you wanted to delete the last two numbers, you would simply remove the last two entries from the stack.

Using a stack to store information has other advantages. Recursion of information is one. The term "recursion" basically refers to the ability to determine a succession of elements (such as stack elements) by referring to one or more of the elements already generated.

Even though recursion may sound like a weird process, it really is simple. You've probably seen a picture that shows a man sitting in front of a television, whose picture shows a man sitting in front of a television, and so forth. That is just one form that recursion may take.

To cite one simple example of recursion using the stack, pretend for a moment that you wished to generate the powers of two (2×2 is 4, 2×4 is 8, 2×8 is 16, and so forth). You could do so in FORTH with the simple word {POWERS}.

[: POWERS dup 2 * ;]

What this FORTH word does is to duplicate the top element on the stack ({DUP}), place a two on the stack, then multiply the two numbers and leave the result on the stack for the next time you use the word {POWERS}. If the FORTH syntax bothers you at this point, don't worry; just try to grasp the concept that each succeeding element on the stack makes reference to something already on the stack, a simple recursion.

To cite another example of how using a stack is different from using variables to store information, a common problem associated with using variables is one called "garbage collection." This inelegant term refers to the process of reclaiming memory space no longer needed, as in the case of a variable that is no longer in use (or when the information contained in the variable uses less space than the data stored there previously).

The stack concept has its own built-in garbage collection. When you remove an item from the stack for use, its space is reclaimed automatically by FORTH. This results in two advantages, one of speed (some garbage-collection routines in other languages take an immense amount of time — to the computer — to function) and one of convenience (you are not left with any information in memory that you might later have to contend with).

What's in the Stack

In almost every existing version of FORTH, each element of the stack consists of two bytes of information. In other words, each element consists of 16 bits of information.

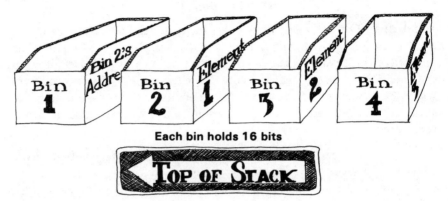

Each bin holds 16 bits

Information is normally stored in a single-stack element in two ways. The first is called a 16-bit signed number, and the second is called a 16-bit unsigned number.

You'll learn more about the distinction between signed and unsigned numbers later, but the basic difference to a programmer lies in the range of numbers each can address.

TYPE	RANGE
(15 bits + sign)	
signed numbers	-32768 to 32767
(16 bits)	
unsigned numbers	0 to 65535

Since these ranges are extremely limited, another method of stored information on the stack is also implemented in FORTH. "Double numbers" are numbers that consist of two FORTH stack elements considered together (for example, two 16-bit elements or 32 bits).

One 16-bit stack element

One 32-bit stack element

Double numbers can also be signed and unsigned.

TYPE	RANGE
signed double numbers (31 bits + sign)	-2147483648 to 2147483647
unsigned double numbers (32 bits)	0 to 4294967296

FORTH does not change the size of the stack to deal with double numbers. Instead, a double number is made up of two stack elements. You must keep track of which numbers on the stack are double and which are single elements, and use the appropriate functions to manipulate them.

It should also be mentioned that there are ways to manipulate half an element on the stack at a time. Half of 16 bits is a normal "byte" of information.

In short, the FORTH stack consists of 16-bit elements, but there are ways for you to make FORTH deal with either two elements at a time (double numbers) or only half an element at a time (bytes). Unfortunately, some of the useful stack-manipulation words FORTH contains cannot be used on bytes of information. FORTH can deal directly only with the top byte on the stack at a time (although you can always invent your own functions to deal with the second byte from the top, should you need direct access to it).

Representing the Stack

Since the stack is a key ingredient in FORTH, you'll want to be able to see exactly how the stack is manipulated thoughout this text.

A visual method will be used to illustrate what you type in FORTH and its effect on the stack. Since you can do many things with elements of the stack, it is important that you recognize that almost every function can be reduced to one of the following basic building blocks:

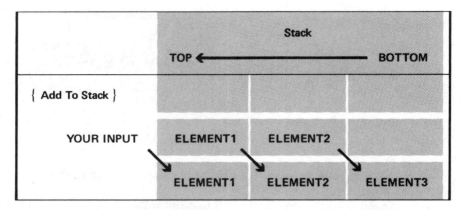

What you type (if it isn't a FORTH word) becomes the new ELE-MENT1, and everything that was on the stack is pushed back one. If you typed a FORTH word, the result of that word's function will be added to the top of the stack.

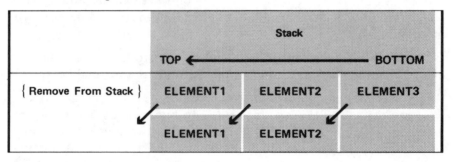

What you typed caused one element to be removed from the stack, with everything else moving up one position.

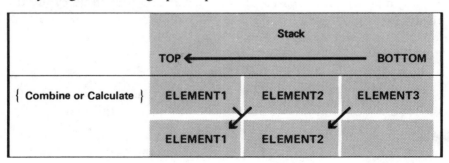

Your typing causes the combination of two (or more) of the elements on the stack. An example would be typing {+}. This tells FORTH to take the top two elements off the stack, add them together, and store the result as the new top element.

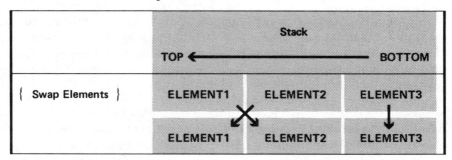

In this example, FORTH has swapped two elements on the stack while leaving a third untouched. (Some FORTH operations swap more than two elements, but the principle shown above remains the same.)

A form of the previous notation will be used throughout this book. An example of a real series of FORTH operations follows.

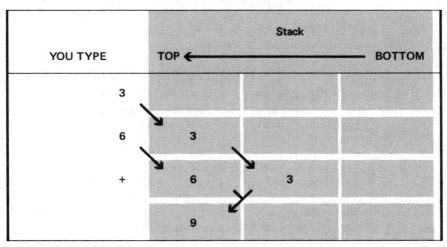

(Note: Appendix A is a blank sheet of coding paper that utilizes this scheme.)

You should note that this book uses a different method of representing the stack than that which you'll find in most FORTH manuals. Generally, the FORTH stack is represented with the top on the right and the bottom on the left.

That's fine, but you're reading from left to right and expecting information in the order you'll use it to form conclusions. The representation used in this book should help simplify your learning process. Afterward, you can learn to think backward like most FORTH documenters.

A second convention you won't find used in this book is the "shorthand" method (found in most FORTH manuals and the Glossary of this book) to represent what elements of the stack are used by what words. This shorthand format looks something like the following:

elements WORD elements

↙   ↘

**the stack before   the stack after
WORD is executed   WORD is executed**

This convention uses the following abbreviations:

**n = 16-bit signed number
u = 16-bit unsigned number
d = 32-bit signed double number
ud = 32-bit unsigned double number
addr = memory address (16 bits)
byte = byte value (8 bits)
c = seven-bit ASCII character in a one-byte field
flag = Boolean (true/false) value**

Thus, a word that takes two numbers off the stack and replaces them with a third would be represented like the following:

n2 n1 WORD n3

This means that the word uses "n1" and "n2" (in that order) to create "n3," which becomes the top element in the stack.

The shorthand notation, helpful for reference purposes, is used only in the appendices of this book. The simplification gets in the way of understanding what is happening for newcomers to FORTH, so the expanded representation previously described will be used throughout the text. An expanded representation of the example word shown earlier looks like the following:

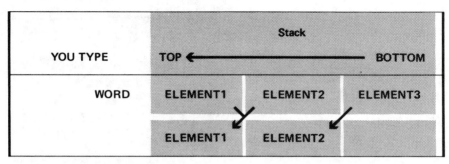

This representation graphically shows where each element on the stack goes during the operation and should prove less confusing to newcomers to FORTH.

Some Definitions

A great number of predefined FORTH words manipulate the stack. As you will learn eventually, you can combine these words to create new stack manipulations. For now, however, concentrate on learning the following basic manipulators:

(Description)	WORD	Stack		
		TOP ←		BOTTOM
{ DROP } removes one element from the stack	DROP	X	Y	Z
N1 DROP		Y	Z	
{ SWAP } exchanges the top two elements on the stack	SWAP	X	Y	Z
N2 N1 SWAP N1 N2		Y	X	Z
{ DUP } duplicates the top element on the stack	DUP	X	Y	
N1 DUP N1 N2		X	X	Y

(Description)	WORD	Stack TOP ← BOTTOM		
{ OVER } duplicates the second element on the stack **N2 N1 OVER N2 N1 N2**	OVER	X / Y	Y / X	Y
{+ − *} or {/} performs the arithmetic function specified on the top two elements on stack **N2 N1 + N(1+2)**	+	X / Y	X+Y Z	Z

Other FORTH words allow you to manipulate the 32-bit double words (two stack elements) in one step. An example of this might be the following:

(Description)	WORD	Stack TOP ← BOTTOM					
{ 2DUP } duplicates the double number on the stack **D1 2DUP D1 D2** **N2 N1 2DUP N2 N1 N2 N1**	2DUP	A	B	X	Y		
		A	B	A	B	X	Y

Appendix B is a list of FORTH words and their effects on the stack. You'll find that new words will be introduced throughout this book as they prove necessary, but, if for some reason you need to find the action of a specific word before it is introduced, check Appendix B.

Where Is the Stack

In most versions of FORTH, the stack starts at the top of available free memory and works its way down in memory as the stack grows. An internal (to FORTH) pointer is kept that stores the address of the current top stack entry.

Unfortunately, some stacks grow up instead of down. You'll have to check your manual to see which yours does.

However, most versions of FORTH provide you with a word — {SP@} — that, when executed, places the stack's old address on the stack. If that sounds confusing to you, examine the following illustration:

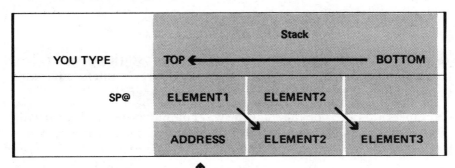

The address of previous ELEMENT1

In your system's memory, the above situation would look something like this:

Okay, but where's the bottom of the stack? To solve this, you use the FORTH words {S0} and {@}. Executing these words in order will place the address of the initial value (that is, the first memory location used for the stack) of the stack onto the stack. The illustration of its use looks just like that of {SP@}, with the substitution of {S0} {@} for {SP@}.

Stacks of Characters

So far, the fact that the stack is of use only for storing numbers has been implied. That's true, but remember that computers internally represent characters as binary numbers (see Appendix C).

Numbers are stored on the stack the way computers generally deal with them (that is, in binary form). If you tried to print a binary number directly onto your display, it wouldn't work, and you'd most likely get some nonsensical display. Wouldn't it be nice if you could print out the numbers stored on the stack as Arabic numbers? Well, you can.

To get the data off the stack and onto the screen in numbers you understand, you use the "dot" command ({.}). Typing a period will have the same result as the {DROP} word does, but it will also display the Arabic number that was on the stack on your console display.

Sometimes you want to have the ASCII equivalent of the number displayed on your screen (as in the case of letters). To do this, you use the {EMIT} function. If there is a decimal 65 on the stack and you type {EMIT}, an "A" will be displayed on your console device because 65 is the decimal value for an "A" using the ASCII encoding scheme (see Appendix C). If you typed {.} instead of {EMIT}, you would see the number "65" displayed on your screen, not the letter "A."

Summary

Later in this book you'll learn other ways to get things on and off the main FORTH stack. But for now, let's summarize what you've learned so far:

- The stack is a pile of information.

- Using a stack has advantages, including speed, convenience, array processing, recursion, and garbage collection.

- Stacks usually consist of 16-bit elements which can be signed numbers (-32768 to 32767) or unsigned numbers (0 to 65535).

- Sometimes stacks contain double numbers (32 bits) which can be signed (-2147483648 to 2147483647) or unsigned numbers (0 to 4294967296).

- The basic stack manipulations are adding something to the stack, removing something from the stack, combining elements on the stack, and exchanging elements on the stack.

- The stack often starts at the top of memory and works its way down, while versions do the opposite.

In addition, you've run into several stack-manipulation words including the following:

- DROP removes top element from the stack.

- DUP duplicates the top element on the stack.

- OVER duplicates the second element on the stack.

- 2DUP duplicates the top two elements on the stack.

- SWAP exchanges top two elements on the stack.

- + adds the top two elements on the stack.

- - subtracts the top element from the second element on the stack.

- * multiplies the top two elements on the stack.

- / divides the second element by the top element on the stack.

- SP@ places the address of the top element of the stack onto the stack.

- . displays in Arabic numbers on the display the binary value of the top element on the stack.

- EMIT displays the top element on the stack according to its ASCII equivalent.

Last, you've seen how this book will display the effect of the stack and FORTH words on the stack, and how it may be represented in the manual that accompanies your version of FORTH.

Chapter 4

FORTH
Arithmetic

"Two plus two isn't possible in FORTH."
anonymous

By the time you've finished this chapter, you should be well versed in the unusual method with which FORTH handles arithmetic operations.

The Post-Fix Is In

If you learned math in the traditional manner, you were probably brainwashed into thinking that two plus two is four.

Computers don't believe that. To a slice of silicon, most arithmetic operations are performed in something commonly known as "post-fix" notation.

Post-fix rules say that you must state the operands before stating the operations to be performed. In other words, you state the numbers and then the operation to be performed.

2 + 2   becomes   2 2 +

The fact that the mathematical operation is specified last led to the name post-fix.

Actually, post-fix notation is also referred to as reverse Polish notation. As "The Software Works FORTH" manual explains, the term "Polish" comes from "an attempt by a largely English-speaking computer science community to credit the origins of the technique without undertaking the risky task of attempting to pronounce [the name of the inventor, Polish logician Jan] Lukaciewicz."

Lukaciewicz's system is used quite extensively today in electronic equipment, most notably in Hewlett-Packard calculators, Pascal compilers, and, yes, FORTH.

Getting a Post-Fix or Forget Parentheses

If you flunked high school algebra, you may be in real trouble when you begin calculating with FORTH. Then again, it may help.

Perhaps you remember some of the following rules of evaluating algebraic expressions:

1. Do all multiplication and division before addition and subtraction operations.

$$A + B + C * D + E + F + G$$
↑
calculated first

2. Calculate the expressions in the innermost set of parentheses first.

$$(A + (B * C + (D / E)))$$
↑
calculated first

Continue working out, one set of parentheses at a time.

3. Work from left to right if none of the above rules applies.

$$A + B + C + D + E$$
↑
calculated first

Using the rules listed above, if you were given the expression

$$(24 * 5) / 2 - 5 + 10$$

to calculate, you'd perform the following steps:

1. multiply 24 times 5   (subtotal equals 120)

2. divide by 2   (subtotal equals 60)

3. subtract 5   (subtotal equals 55)

4. add 10   (total equals 65)

In the language BASIC, this calculation could be stated in the following manner:

$$24 * 5 / 2 - 5 * 10$$

Note that the operators appear between the numbers they work with.

FORTH's reverse Polish notation changes the way you write the operators. In FORTH the same calculation would appear as

$$24 \; 5 * 2 / 5 - 10 +$$

This is sufficiently different so that you might want to have

1. **24 5 * 2 / 5 - 10 +**   24 and 5 are the first numbers to work with; multiplication is the operation to perform.

2. **245 * 2 / 5 - 10 +**   The result of the previous operation and 2 are the numbers to work with; division is the operation to perform.

3. **245 * 2 / 5 - 10 +**   The result of the previous operation and 5 are the numbers to work with; subtraction is the operation to perform.

4. **245 * 2 / 5 - 10 +**   The result of the previous operation and 10 are the numbers to work with; addition is the operation to perform.

If you know a little about FORTH, you'll know that the numbers have been rearranged from the way most FORTH programmers would state the equation. Just as with regular algebraic mathematics, there are several ways to write the same functionally equivalent calculation.

You've been intentionally shown the calculations in a rather logical fashion. FORTH programmers generally leave numbers strewn all over the stack and put together a string of operators at the last minute that miraculously perform the calculation. Just so that you game lovers will have something to scratch your head about, here's a sample of the way a typical FORTH programmer might tackle a more involved expression:

algebraic: 25 + 6 + 4 * (5 + 3 + 1 * 311)
FORTH: 25 6 + 4 5 3 + 1 311 * + * +

Notice the way the four operators pop up at the end of the equation. Since the common operators of addition, subtraction, multiplication, and division all work on two numbers at a time in FORTH, it seems curious that four operations would just sit there by themselves. (HINT: If you haven't figured it out yet, read the next chapter and carefully plot out what's on the stack at any given moment during the above calculation.)

Actually, a veteran FORTH programmer probably wouldn't have made the direct conversion between algebraic and post-fix notation shown above. Instead, he or she would have written something like the following:

25 6 4 311 5 3 1 + + * * + +

After programming in FORTH for a while, you'll most likely develop similar tendencies.

─────It's His FORTH Operation, Doctor─────

You've been briefly introduced to the common arithmetic operators. In fact, you shouldn't have any trouble recognize {+}, {-}, {*}, and {/} as representing addition, subtraction, multiplication, and division.

Each of the four basic operators works in the same manner, combining two stack elements as presented in the last chapter. You'll remember the basic form was the following:

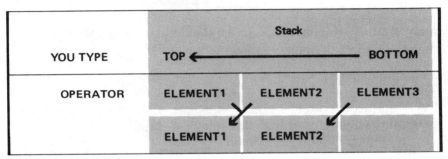

Let's modify that from its general form to a more specific one.

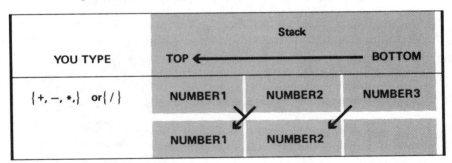

This means that the specified operation combines the top two numbers on the stack, resulting in a new single number on the top of the stack. Everything else on the stack moves up one position.

The result of a division — {/} — is sequence dependent (what divides into what?); in FORTH, a division is performed by dividing the second number in the stack by the first.

A special warning: Each of the basic operators assumes that the numbers on the stack are single numbers, signed or unsigned. If you've mixed in some double numbers, read on.

What's the Point

So far, you've only learned about single-integer numbers. You'll remember, however, that something called "double numbers" was mentioned in an earlier chapter.

In most versions of FORTH, the way you tell the language to use double numbers (32 bits) is to type a decimal point in the number. It doesn't matter where the decimal point is, as standard FORTH uses only integer numbers for calculations.

Thus, the following numbers are all the same in FORTH:

19.81   1.981   00000.1981

Double-Number Operators

The operators for double-number calculations are distinctly different from those already mentioned for single numbers.

Instead of using {+}, double numbers use {D+} for addition. The subtraction of double numbers requires a {D-} instead of a {-}. Double numbers have no operators for multiplication or division.

So that you can compare double-number operations to those of single numbers, here's what the stack representation looks like:

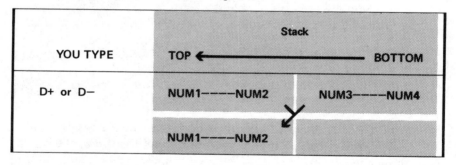

YOU TYPE	Stack	
	TOP ←	BOTTOM
D+ or D−	NUM1——NUM2	NUM3——NUM4
	NUM1——NUM2	

The linking (hyphens) between numbers on the stack in this representation signifies that these are double numbers (which take up two stack elements instead of one).

FORTH doesn't remind you which numbers on the stack are double and which are single, so throughout this book every single number will be shown, with double numbers indicated by linking two singles together, as in the above example.

Mixed Numbers, Anyone

It is possible to mix single and double numbers in several arithmetic operations.

You could, for example, multiply two single numbers together and store the result in a double number. The operator for this procedure is called {M*}.

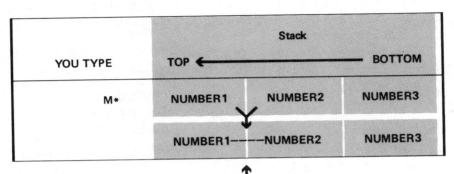

a double number result

Another "mixed-mode" operation is called {M/}, which means to divide a double number by a single number. This is a special operation because, unlike with the other integer operations in FORTH, both the quotient (the number to the left of the decimal point) and the remainder are left on the stack as single numbers for you to use.

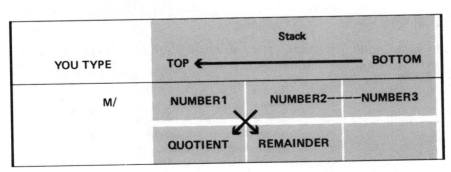

There are other mixed-mode operations, and some versions of FORTH have extended the language by adding still more. For now, these operations should be enough to get you started.

Words for the Operators

So far the expression "operator" has been used to refer to arithmetic functions to be performed upon two numbers. This has been done so that you will understand that a mathematical calculation is taking place.

In actuality, each of the operators described so far in this chapter is a FORTH word (that is, executable function). Keep this in mind, because you'll need this concept when you learn more about words and their uses in the next chapter.

Your Number's Up

You've now examined the basic concepts of FORTH arithmetic. If you think back to what you've read, you should recognize the following key information:

• Post-fix (or reverse Polish notation) always states the mathematical operation after the numbers to be acted upon have been stated.

• Traditional algebraic notation allows complex formulas to be expressed out of order; FORTH notation requires that one operation be done at a time; thus, complex formulas generally are written in the order of calculation.

• Double numbers are 32 bits (two stack elements) in length and are created by using a "." within a number.

• Mixed-mode operations are calculations that use both single and double numbers.

• You should also now recognize the following FORTH words introduced in this chapter:

Word	Operation
+	single-number addition
-	single-number subtraction
*	single-number multiplication
/	single-number division
D+	double-number addition
D-	double-number subtraction
M*	mixed-mode multiplication
M/	mixed-mode division

Chapter 5

Using
FORTH

" . . . and stringing pretty words that make no sense."
Browning, Aurora Leigh, Book I

It's time to stop reading about FORTH and begin to use it. In this chapter, you'll be introduced to some basic principles, which, with what has already been presented, should allow you to begin making FORTH work for you.

Venturing FORTH

If you have a version of FORTH for your computer, now's the time to get it out and begin to use it. If you don't have a version of FORTH handy, at least use a piece of paper to keep track of the stack.

It's impossible to tell you exactly how to get FORTH running on your computer, because there are so many different computers and versions of FORTH. Make sure you know how to get FORTH into the memory of your computer, waiting for commands. Usually, this involves typing one of the following statements, or something similar:

FORTH
GO FORTH
RUN FORTH
LOAD FORTH

Most versions of FORTH will identify themselves when they have been properly loaded into memory and are executing correctly. You'll probably see something like

```
Mythical FORTH Version 1.1

Ok
```

The "OK" informs you that FORTH is ready and waiting for you to tell it what to do. At least one version of FORTH, SL5 from the Stackworks, uses the prompt ">" instead.

You're ready to begin.

Stack 'Em Up and Pull 'Em Off

One thing you need to know is how to get things on and off the stack. Remember that the stack will hold only numbers.

To put something on the stack, simply type the number you want stored there.

```
Mythical FORTH Version 1.1

Ok


32<CR>Ok
```

In the previous example, you typed a 32 followed by a carriage return (the convention of representing the use of the carriage return key "<CR>" will be used throughout this book). FORTH replied "OK" to indicate it was ready for the next command. If you were to look at the stack now, you would find that there was one item on it, a "32." Remember that the 32 is stored in binary form, using 16 bits (two bytes) of memory space.

In that example, two other conventions were used in addition to that of the "<CR>" representing your pressing the carriage return key. Those conventions are that anything FORTH types will appear in normal lettering, and anything you type will appear underlined.

You could continue to put items on the stack by entering more numbers. You do not have to enter a carriage return after each one. FORTH recognizes the different numbers only if they are separated by spaces, however.

```
Mythical FORTH Version 1.1

Ok


32<CR>Ok

14 12 13 1 10000 1<CR>Ok
```

In this example you have entered six more numbers, all of which are now on the stack. If you were to take a snapshot of the stack right now, it would look like the following:

TOP	**1**
	10000
	1
	13
	12
	14
BOTTOM	**32**

Getting numbers onto the stack is easy, but there are numerous ways to get them off.

If you want FORTH to parrot the number on the stack (that is, recite it exactly as you entered it), you use a period — {.}, called a "dot" — to get numbers off.

```
Mythical FORTH Version 1.1

Ok


32<CR>Ok

14 12 13 1 10000 1<CR>Ok

.<CR>1 Ok
```

Now, you have typed a dot followed by a carriage return. FORTH has "popped" the top element off the stack and displayed its value on your console display. The stack now contains only six elements, since you've removed the seventh one.

If you're wondering about double numbers, you can retrieve them, too, in a similar fashion. To remove and display the top double number on the stack (two stack elements), you use {D.} —called "D-dot" — instead of the dot command listed previously.

A Bit of Character

The answer is "yes," characters can be manipulated. The secret is the fact that characters are stored internally as a code by the computer. Can you get them on and off the stack, too?

The answer is "yes," characters can be manipulated. The secret is the fact that characters are stored internally as a code by the computer. Specifically, FORTH uses ASCII code to store characters. Given a chart that shows all the characters and their values in ASCII, you can enter and remove letters and special characters. Table 5-1 contains a partial listing of ASCII-coded characters.

TABLE 5-1. PARTIAL ASCII CHART[1]

33 = !	34 = "	35 = #	36 = $
37 = %	38 = &	39 = '	40 = (
41 =)	42 = *	43 = +	44 = ,
45 = -	46 = .	47 = /	48 = Ø
49 = 1	50 = 2	51 = 3	52 = 4
53 = 5	54 = 6	55 = 7	56 = 8
57 = 9	58 = :	59 = ;	60 = <
61 = =	62 = >	63 = ?	64 = @
65 = A	66 = B	67 = C	68 = D
69 = E	70 = F	71 = G	72 = H
73 = I	74 = J	75 = K	76 = L
77 = M	78 = N	79 = O	80 = P
81 = Q	82 = R	83 = S	84 = T
85 = U	86 = V	87 = W	88 = X
89 = Y	90 = Z		

To put a letter on the stack, you could either enter its numeric value (by looking it up in an ASCII table) or use a special input statement called {KEY}.

When executed, {KEY} waits for you to type a character and stores its ASCII value on the stack. Thus, getting a letter onto the stack is a two-step process. You type {KEY} to put FORTH into the input mode, and then you type the character you wish saved on the stack.

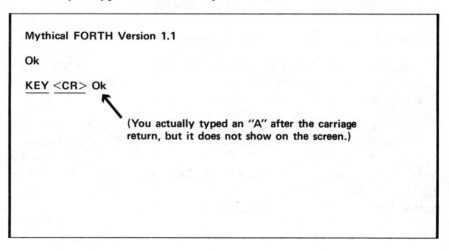

Mythical FORTH Version 1.1

Ok

KEY <CR> Ok

(You actually typed an "A" after the carriage return, but it does not show on the screen.)

---

[1]A full listing appears in Appendix C.

What is stored on the stack in the above example is a decimal 65, whose ASCII code value is "A." If you use the dot command to remove the top stack element, you can verify this.

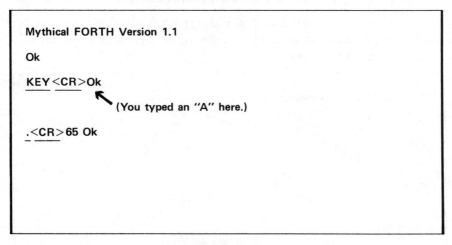

To remove the top number on the stack as the character it represents, you use the {EMIT} command. {EMIT} takes the top element of the stack and displays it on the screen using the ASCII equivalent of its value.

If you know something about ASCII code, you know that it uses only seven bits of information to represent the entire character set. FORTH stack elements contain 16 bits. {EMIT} uses only the seven least significant bits in figuring out what character to display.

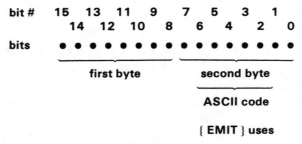

In other words, {EMIT} doesn't care what the first nine bits in the stack element to be displayed are.

——————Don't Just Sit There, Do Something——————

Okay, now that you know how to get things onto and off the stack, it is time to combine that knowledge with some basic FORTH words.

You'll remember from the last chapter that FORTH arithmetic requires that the numbers be on the stack before an operator is invoked. Let's add 2 and 2.

```
Mythical FORTH Version 1.1

Ok

2 2 + .<CR> 4 Ok
```

Just to make sure that you didn't get lost, take a look at the following diagram of what is happening at each step:

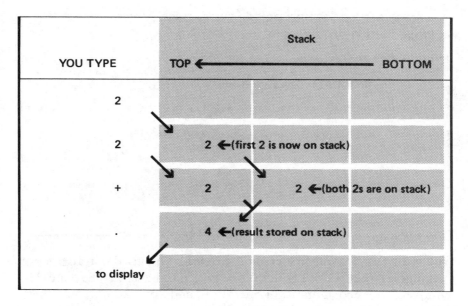

In other words, each "2" went onto the stack. The addition operation combined the top two numbers on the stack and stored the result as the new top number on the stack. The dot command removed that number and displayed it.

If the above notation is still a little bit confusing to you, think of each horizontal line as a "snapshot" of what is happening at a specific moment in time. The line that has "+ 2 2" on it shows you that at the moment you type {+}, the stack has a pair of 2s on it. At the moment you type {.}, the stack has a "4" on it.

To Err is Human

Just for the fun of it, try typing another plus sign after the first one in the above example (remember to leave a space between each FORTH entry). You should now see something like the following:

```
Mythical FORTH Version 1.1

Ok

2 2 + + . .<CR> 8246 .? The stack is empty.
```

You've just made your first error. The reason you get the strange error message is that FORTH requires two numbers on the stack to complete the second addition operation, and you had only one there (the "4" from the first addition).

Actually, in the version of FORTH used to generate the example, it was not the extra addition that caused the error message, but the second dot command (as evidenced by the ".?" message, FORTH couldn't understand the dot). The "8246," which certainly isn't the value of 2 2 +, comes from the fact that you attempted to add with only one number on the stack. If you ever begin to get strange results in simple arithmetic calculations, the first thing to suspect is that there weren't as many elements on the stack as you thought there were.

Error messages abound in FORTH and you can usually modify them to your heart's content (more on that later).

More Words

It's time to accelerate the pace a bit. At this point, you should have a general idea about FORTH arithmetic, the execution of words, and how the stack is used. You're now going to be introduced to some new vocabulary so that you can try out a few ideas of your own.

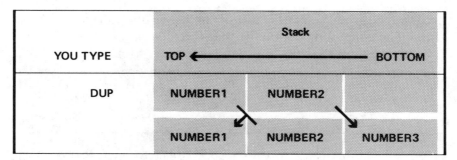

{DUP}: duplicates the top number on the stack. In other words, what was the top element on the stack is now the top two elements on the stack.

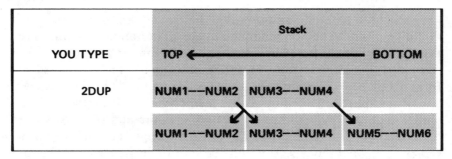

{2DUP}: duplicates the top double number on the stack. In other words, what was the top two elements on the stack is now the top repeated so that it is the top four elements on the stack.

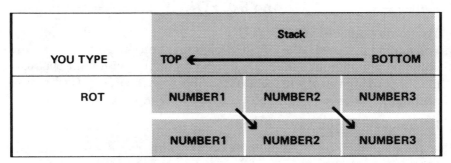

{ROT}: rotates the third element on the stack up to the first position, while shifting the other two elements back one. This is a method of getting the top two elements out of the way while working with the third. The conclusion should be that three consecutive {ROT}s will leave the stack in the same position you started with.

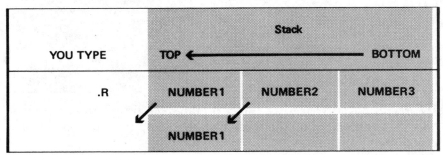

{.R}: the "dot-R" command removes the second number on the stack and displays it on the screen much as the dot command displays the top number. The difference is that the first number on the stack is a "formatting field;" it tells FORTH how many spaces to use for formatting the second number. A {.R} with a pair of 2s on the stack will send out a space followed by a 2 (no leading zeros are emitted). A {.R} with a pair of 3s on the stack will send to the console two spaces followed by a 3. This command is useful for aligning numbers on the screen in printed reports. You must be careful, however, to make sure that you specify a formatting field that is as wide as the longest number, or else you may find that the numbers no longer line up.

And So, FORTH

You're now an official FORTH user. Remember, at this point you know quite a number of FORTH words that you can type and execute immediately on your system. You should practice with your accumulated knowledge until you feel comfortable with the FORTH stack and arithmetic processes before moving on to the next chapter.

In this chapter, you have learned

• How to load and execute FORTH (with some help from the FORTH manual that accompanies your version).

• How to get both numbers and characters on and off the stack.

• How to use the stack for arithmetic calculations.

- What a FORTH error message looks like and why one might occur.

- Some new words, including

.	prints out top number from stack
KEY	inputs a character from the keyboard to the stack
EMIT	displays the ASCII representation of the top number on the stack
DUP	duplicates the top single number on the stack
2DUP	duplicates the top double number on the stack
ROT	rotates the third element on the stack up to the first and moves the top two down one
.R	formats printed numbers using the top two elements of the stack

Chapter 6

Interpreting And Compiling

"Egad, I think the interpreter is
the hardest to be understood of the two!"
Sheridan, The Critic

In this chapter you'll learn about one of the key assets of FORTH, the ability to create new words from existing ones.

Review of Words

Just to make sure that you aren't confused before being introduced to some new concepts, the following is a summary of some of the things you've learned about FORTH words:

• A FORTH word is immediately executable. You type it and it executes. (Actually, it isn't quite that simple. You can, for instance, type a string of FORTH words — each set off from one another by a space — and effectively not execute them until you press the carriage return key.) To a FORTH veteran, the difference is important, but beginners can just assume that words execute after you type them.

• FORTH words perform functions. You've been introduced to several FORTH words so far, which do anything from calculating to rearranging the stack to performing input or output functions.

You'll remember that programming in FORTH is like building a pyramid: you use words to build a higher level block, to build one yet higher, and so on. It's time to find out how to do that.

My Building Blocks, Please

Let's say that you wanted to add two single-digit numbers and then display them on the console screen.

The sequence of FORTH words to perform this sequence of events would be

KEY 48 - KEY 48 - + .

The {48-} after each {KEY} converts each digit from its ASCII code representation to its equivalent numerical value.

Assume, also, that you'd like this new meta-function to be called {ADAMUP}.

To create a new word {ADAMUP}, you need to know how to define your own words in the dictionary. It's actually very simple. All you do is put a colon and the name in front of the sequence of words, and terminate the whole string with a semicolon. Here's how you would define {ADAMUP}:

: ADAMUP KEY 48 - KEY 48 - + . ;

Notice several things about this "colon definition." First, all FORTH words (including the colon, your new word name, and the semicolon) are set apart by at least one space. Second, the sequence is just as you wish it to execute.

Now What

Any time that you want to execute your process, all you type is {ADAMUP}, since it's now in your FORTH dictionary. In fact, you can even use {ADAMUP} in subsequent definitions you create — thus the pyramid programming effect.

When you type a colon into FORTH, it does not actually execute any of the following processes up to the semicolon. Instead, FORTH only checks to see if these words exist and uses their addresses in creating the new word. There are some exceptions to this, but none which you need to worry about at this time.

Compilation in FORTH, therefore, is not what is traditionally called compilation. Normally, to compile something on a computer means to reduce it to machine-language code. In FORTH, it is merely the creation of a new word.

There are many mistakes that you can make in creating colon definitions. You might use a word that doesn't exist, for instance. Appendix E is a list of common FORTH error messages.

Over and Over and Over

Here's something you might not have expected: you can redefine existing words, even those built into your version of FORTH.

The following definition is valid:

: DUP KEY 48 - KEY 48 - + . ;

{DUP} appears in the above example, even though it already has a definition. The new definition will remain until you either reload or restart FORTH or tell it to "forget" that definition (which will be discussed later). FORTH will tell you when you redefine something by presenting the advisory message "ISN'T UNIQUE." You haven't made a mistake, but FORTH is warning you that you've redefined {DUP}.

Other Define Creations

You should be aware of several other FORTH words in conjunction with the colon definitions described above.

{FORGET} name

To delete all dictionary entries that you create after a specific point, simply type the FORTH word {FORGET} followed by the name of the word from which the deletions are made. Let's say that you had created the following new words:

BOB
TED
CAROL
ALICE

If you had created them in the order listed above, typing {FORGET CAROL} will cause FORTH to delete the entries for both {CAROL} and {ALICE}.

{FORGET} should be used with great care. If you create many words, you can easily forget in what order you created them and thus have no idea what the effect of a {FORGET} command might be.

{VLIST}

You may wonder how you can remember what words you have in your dictionary and what order you entered them in. Fortunately, FORTH has a way of finding out.

{VLIST} is a command that displays all of the names of words defined in the context vocabulary. The order in which the words are displayed is exactly the reverse of the order in which you defined them. In other words, the last word you defined will be the first displayed using {VLIST}.

In some versions of FORTH, {CLIST} or {DLIST} performs the same function as {VLIST}. Check your FORTH manual to see if your FORTH might be one of these.

So There You Have It

In this short chapter you learned a big concept — the "colon definitions" which make FORTH such a unique and highly desirable language. You should now be able to create some simple manipulations with your own words and dictionaries.

The following is a summary of the main concepts you learned in this chapter:

• Colon definitions (or compilations) are merely a sequence of words you want executed and to which you assign a unique name.

• You can redefine existing words.

• The new FORTH words or tools you learned include

:	defines words in the FORTH dictionary
;	defines words in the FORTH dictionary
FORGET	deletes dictionary entries
VLIST (or CLIST or DLIST)	displays all words in context dictionary

Chapter 7

Memory Manipulations

"The words of the wise are as gods,
and as nails fastened by the masters of assemblies."
The Bible, Ecclesiastes, XII, II

The primary thrust of this chapter will be to teach you a number of new words, all of which manipulate the memory of your computer.

The Return of the Variable

If you've programmed in another computer language, you're probably used to working with variables. A variable is simply a place in memory reserved for a specific piece of information you want associated with the variable's name. Suppose, for example, that you wanted to keep track of the number of base hits in a baseball game. Wouldn't it be nice if you could create a little "pocket" in memory for that number and retrieve it using the name "HITS"? You can.

To create a variable, you type the word {VARIABLE} followed by the name you wish to assign it.

VARIABLE name

Some versions of FORTH also require you to enter a beginning value for the variable. If your version is one of these, you need to precede the above information with the value, as in the following:

value VARIABLE name

FIG-FORTH takes the top value on the stack and initializes the variable to that value. In other words, it functions exactly as in the example, except that if you don't assign a value, the current value in the top position of the stack is used as the initial value. If you're using FIG-FORTH, or another version of FORTH that operates like this, be careful. You could spend hours trying to find out what's wrong with your FORTH program, only to discover that what you thought was the initial value in a variable actually was not.

When you create a variable, you are actually creating another dictionary entry. Therefore, in choosing a name, you should bear in mind everything in the last chapter that discussed creating words. The difference between a variable and a word in FORTH is primarily that no user-definable executable code is associated with the variable.

Store It and Fetch It

Just creating a variable does you no good; you need to be able to put information into the memory space reserved for the variable and get it back out. The FORTH words that do this for you are called "store" and "fetch."

The first word you need to know is called "store." In FORTH, it is represented by the word {!}. To store something (that is, to use the word {!}), FORTH needs to know two things: the address at which to store the information and the information to be stored there.

To put something into a variable's waiting memory, you place the value on the top of the stack, then type your variable's name (which retrieves its address) followed by a space and {!}.

value   name   !   ← general form
48 CHIMPS   !   ← example

The word {!} doesn't have to be associated with a variable. Typing a variable's name places its address on the top of the stack. Thus, if you peeked inside FORTH to see what's happening, you'd see something like the following:

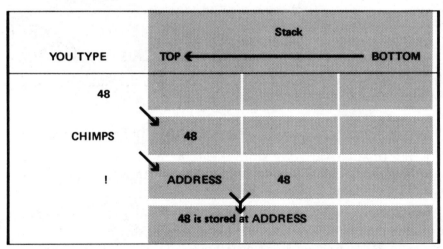

Thus, if you know the numerical designation of the memory address at which you wish to store something, you don't have to create variables at all. You could just as easily have typed

48 4096 !   instead of   48 CHIMPS !

The drawback to your supplying the numerical address is that you must keep track of it and remember it. Basically, it's easier to remember names than numbers, so using variables does make sense in FORTH. Also, if you choose the wrong area of memory, you could easily be storing information in space FORTH is trying to use, so be careful.

Getting information back out of a variable is almost the reverse of {!}. The "fetch" operation (represented by the FORTH word {@}) retrieves information from the address you supply by typing the following variable name:

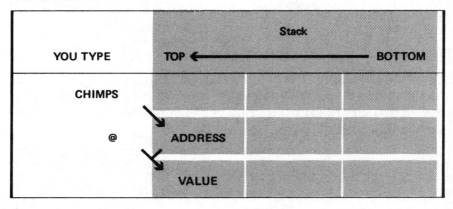

In other words, typing {CHIMPS @} will leave the value associated with the variable {CHIMPS} on the top of the stack.

Constant Reminder

The information variables store is, as the name implies, variable. Another type of information that you can store in memory and reference by name is called a "constant."

Constants are usually defined at the beginning of a program and are usually variables whose value will not change during the course of the program. If you were writing a program to keep track of what happens during a baseball game, for instance, a constant you might want to define would be the number of strikes that make an out.

Constants are defined in FORTH just like variables.

value CONSTANT name ← usual form

or

CONSTANT name ← rare form

If your version of FORTH is like the second type shown in the example, it requires two steps to assign a value to a constant. First you give the constant a name, then you assign it a value. You should always do both steps together (otherwise it is easy to forget to assign a value to the constant, and FORTH will assume it is zero or something worse).

CONSTANT EXAMPLENAME
1234 ' EXAMPLENAME !

The above two lines do the following:

1. Establish a constant called {EXAMPLENAME}.

2. Put the value {1234} on the stack.

3. Typing {'} retrieves the address associated with the word that follows (that is, {EXAMPLENAME}) and puts it on the top of the stack.

4. The {!} operation then places the second value on the stack ({1234}) at the address indicated by the top value on the stack (the address for {EXAMPLENAME}).

Retrieving a constant is a bit different from retrieving a variable. To put the value associated with a constant onto the top of the stack, type the constant's name. You do not need to type {@} in order to retrieve the constant's value. Thus, typing

EXAMPLENAME

after creating the constant would leave the value {1234} on the top of the stack. Remember that with a variable you would have had to type

EXAMPLENAME @

to do the same thing.

─────────Constant Constants and Variables─────────

Most versions of FORTH include some predefined constants and variables. Here's a list of a few of the more common ones and what they're for, but you'll need to consult the manual that came with your FORTH to discover all of the predefined constants and variables you can use.

• {BS} is a predefined constant and stands for "backspace," which has a decimal value of 8 in ASCII code. {BS} always leaves this value on the stack.

• {BL} is a predefined constant and stands for "blank." It leaves the decimal value of 32 (ASCII "blank") on the stack.

• {SCR} is a predefined variable and is associated with the FORTH editor. It leaves the value of the last screen number edited or listed (you'll learn about editors in a later chapter) on the stack.

• {S0} is a predefined variable that contains the address of the initial memory location of the stack. If your version of FORTH does not have a word that tells you how many elements are on the stack, you can easily create such a word by using the following definition:

```
: DEPTH S0 @ SP@ - 2 / 1- ;
```

This will leave the number of elements as the new top element on the stack. This may not work correctly for stacks that grow up instead of down, however.

Some versions of FORTH define a number of other constants and variables. "The Software Works FORTH," for instance, defines the following additional constants and variables: B/BUF, BLK, BLKRW, BSX, C/L, COLUMN, CONSOLE, CONTEXT, CSP, CURFCB, CURRENT, DENSITY, DISK-ERROR, DP, DPL, DWL, DRIVE, DRIVECAP, DRIVEMAP, FENCE, FILENAME, FIRST, HEIGHT, HLD, >IN, INDEV, INMAP, LIMIT, LOGDEV, MODEM, NETWORK, OUTDEV, OUTMAP, PREV, PRINTER, PUNCH, R#, R0, READER, RESET, ROW, RUB, SERIAL#, SHIFT, STATE, SYSDATE, SYSFCB, SYSTIME, TIB, TOF, ULIMIT, UNEXT, USE, VOC-LINK, WARNING, WIDTH.

It is impossible and unnecessary to define all of these constants and variables within the limited space of this book. The same principle applies to each. You type the name, and a value is left on the stack when you're working with constants. You type the name followed by {@} and a value is left on the stack when you're working with variables. To put a new value into a variable you type the new value, the variable's name and {!}. Remember, what a constant or variable is keeping track of may be a value, a double number value, or an address. Again, your manual should tell you everything you need to know about each of these FORTH words.

Movin' On

One of FORTH's nicer attributes is the ability to manipulate large blocks of memory with a single word. The most basic things you might want to do with a section of memory are:

move it	FORTH word {CMOVE}
change it	FORTH word {FILL}
clear it	FORTH word {ERASE}
or display it	FORTH words {CDUMP} and {TYPE}

Moving a section of memory is simple — just place the beginning address of the section you wish to move on the stack, followed by the beginning address of the place you wish it to be and the number of bytes of memory involved. If that sounds hard to conceptualize, just examine the following illustration:

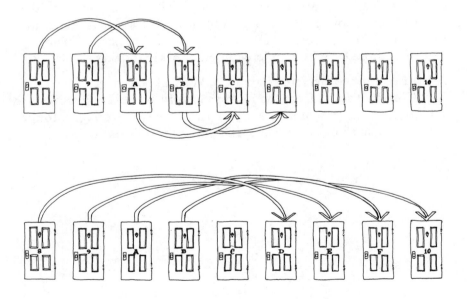

If you wished to move 128 bytes from location 2048 to location 4096 in memory, you'd type the following:

2048   **4096**   **128**   **CMOVE**

FORTH operation

# of bytes to move

starting address of new location

starting address of current location

As you already know, typing these three numbers places them on the stack so that when {CMOVE} comes along, they are used in the reverse of the order you typed them in (remember, the stack is memory that seems to work backward).

There is no reason why you couldn't use some formula to calculate each number involved instead of just typing the numbers. In fact, as you get better at programming in FORTH, you'll let the computer do more of the work.

The {CMOVE} operation works on bytes of memory. There is a {MOVE} operation in FORTH as well. It operates exactly the same way as {CMOVE}, except that it moves 16-bit "chunks" of memory instead of those 8-bit bytes microcomputer programmers are used to.

One other thing to remember about {CMOVE} before we move on is that {CMOVE} starts from the lowest memory address and works its way up. If the section of memory you want to move overlaps into the place you wish to put it, things aren't going to work out right.

If you think about it long enough, you'll see that when FORTH gets to the starting address of the section to which you are copying, it will already have changed that memory. Thus, you didn't really move the block intact — there's going to be a garbled part at the end. If you need to move a block that has overlapping sections, you'll need to create a new FORTH word (see Appendix F for an example).

To put a specific value in a section of memory, you use a command similar to {CMOVE} called {FILL}. You need to specify the following three things to {FILL}:

1. Starting address of memory to fill.

2. The number of bytes to fill.

3. The value (byte) to place in the block of memory defined.

Thus, if you wanted to place the value 145 in all memory from 100 to 110, you'd type

100 10 145 FILL

{FILL} also works from bottom to top, but since nothing is being moved, you don't have to worry about this operation not performing properly.

One thing that should be mentioned at this point is that FORTH nomenclature, especially as software developers create new versions and add their "dream goodies" onto the language, is not very consistent in naming conventions. Why is the byte-oriented {CMOVE} command prefaced by a "C" while the byte-oriented {FILL} command isn't?

The point to note is that when you define new words, you should endeavor to be consistent in your naming practices.

If you wish to clear a section of memory of the values stored there, you need to write zeros into that area. You could do that using the {FILL} command just discussed.

START NUMBER-OF-BYTES 0 FILL

A better way to do this is the {ERASE} command. You specify the starting address and the number of bytes, but the zero is assumed.

START NUMBER-OF-BYTES ERASE ← **general form**
1024 256 ERASE ← **example (put zeros in 256 bytes**
of memory beginning at 1024)

Perhaps instead of modifying memory you just want to see what's there. For this action you'd use {CDUMP}. Alternatively, you could use the {TYPE} command.

{CDUMP} requires that a starting address and the number of bytes to dump are on the stack. Then it will print the values of the stored items in the specified area on your console display.

START NUMBER-OF-BYTES CDUMP ← **general form**
45 324 CDUMP ← **example (dump 324 bytes of**
memory beginning at location 45)

Just like the other functions discussed in this section, {CDUMP} can be executed with numbers calculated from other operations and stored on the stack (make sure you get them in the right order, though).

Also, you can use the form {DUMP} instead of {CDUMP} should you wish to see the contents of 16-bit memory (the stack, for instance). It functions exactly the same way except that it displays the contents of a pair of 8-bit locations.

The following two "dumps" illustrate some of the differences between {DUMP} and {CDUMP}:

```
Mythical FORTH Version 1.1

Ok

1000 10 CDUMP<CR>114 209 35 115 35 114

195 47 3 129 Ok

1000 10 DUMP<CR>53618 29475 29219 12227

33027 53961 63235 10755 530 9054 Ok
```

One last point about {DUMP} and {CDUMP} is that they both display the contents of memory as numbers in the current "base." You'll find out more about changing the number base in FORTH later. For now, unless you have a strange version of FORTH or have been tinkering with things that haven't yet been discussed, everything you see and do should be represented in standard decimal numbers.

───────── Fetchin' and Storin' Part Two ─────────

You already know about storing and fetching information in variables and constants. Most hard-core FORTH programmers use variables sparingly, however.

One of the features of FORTH that often attracts programmers is that the language puts you close to the "guts" of the computer. It is quite possible to manipulate individual memory locations from FORTH without going through the convention of giving them names.

You've just learned about {CMOVE}, {FILL}, {ERASE}, and {CDUMP}, but all of these operations work with blocks (sections) of memory. How about if you just want to play with one location at a time?

Well, you're back to learning about {@} and {!}. These two operations do not need to be associated with variables. Indeed, if you look carefully at what happens when you type

VARIABLENAME @

you'll find that typing {VARIABLENAME} places an address — that of the variable's location — on the stack, while typing {@} replaces the address with the value stored there.

The store operation works similarly. Typing

VALUE VARIABLENAME !

places two values on the stack — first the value to be stored and then the address at which to store it. The {!} stores the value in that address and removes both from the stack.

There is another FORTH word that performs something like the {!} operation, but combines it with {.}. This word is {?}. In fact, even if your version of FORTH doesn't contain {?}, you can simulate it by typing

```
: ? @ . ;
```

You can generalize the fetch and store operations like

ADDRESS @ ←   general form to retrieve information from a memory location

VALUE ADDRESS ← general form to store a value in a memory location

Don't forget that the {@} and {!} operations work with 16-bit memory locations — two bytes in most microcomputers. If you wish to manipulate 32-bit or 8-bit memory locations, you'll need to know about "son-of-fetch," "son-of-store," "father fetch," and "father store" (just kidding, but maybe that will help you remember the idea).

- C@ is used to fetch values from a single byte of memory (8 bits)

- @ is used to fetch values from a normal FORTH memory location (16 bits).

- 2@ is used to fetch values from a double FORTH memory location (32 bits).

- C! is used to store information in a single byte of memory (8 bits).

- ! is used to store information in a normal FORTH memory location (16 bits).

- 2! is used to store information in a double FORTH memory location (32 bits).

Examine the last of these new instructions, just to make sure you understand the concepts involved.

If you have the following information stored, beginning at memory location 0000

00	32	12	34	12	23	values stored
↓	↓	↓	↓	↓	↓	
00	01	02	03	04	05	memory locations

and if you then type

5. 0 2!

(that is, store the double number 5. at 0) memory would now look like

00	00	05	00	12	23	values stored
↓	↓	↓	↓	↓	↓	
00	01	02	03	04	05	memory locations

The "05" occurs in the third memory position in the above example because of the way the machine being used stores 16-bit numbers (8080, 780, 8086, and PDP 11-based computers reverse the order of the two bytes that make up a single number in FORTH).

(NOTE: This is not true of all implementations of FORTH. You might want to use the following sequence of commands to check how your version of FORTH stores double numbers.)

```
Mythical FORTH Version 1.1

Ok

: showme 4 0 do i C@ . loop ;<CR>Ok

5. 0 2! showme<CR>0 0 5 0 Ok
```

The {2!} operation affected four bytes (32 bits) of memory. FORTH isn't going to stop you from trying to store another 32-bit value at location 0001. If you did so, you would obviously invalidate what you had already stored at location 0000.

Am I Your Type

You may have noticed that the one thing not yet discussed is how to get memory values out onto your display as regular characters instead of values. Actually, you just need to be able to combine two concepts already presented to figure it out. What would the following sequence of FORTH words do, for instance?

ADDRESS C@ EMIT

The answer is that the value stored at the {ADDRESS} would be retrieved and displayed using the ASCII character equivalent to its value.

Using this string of three words could be somewhat cumbersome if you wish to grab and display a whole handful of consecutive memory locations. The FORTH designers realized this and provided you with the word {TYPE}.

{TYPE} requires two numbers on the stack. The bottom number is the address at which to begin; the top number on the stack is the number of bytes to display.

ADDRESS NUMBER-OF-BYTES TYPE ← general form
545 23 TYPE ← example (would display 23 characters
beginning with the one at location 545)

————————More Than You Can Remember————————

Yes, it does sound like a lot of information to remember about memory manipulations, but it really isn't. Take a look at the following things that should have become apparent while reading this chapter:

• There are basically four ways to deal with information in memory: variables, constants, manipulate blocks of memory, and manipulate individual memory locations.

• The basic operations you'll be performing with memory in getting things into it and out of it are:

@ C@ 2@ (fetch memory locations)
! C! 2! (store into memory)

• Some constants and variables are predefined in FORTH.

BS BL SCR S0

(Others may depend on your version of FORTH.)

• With blocks of memory, the basic operations are

move	➔	CMOVE, MOVE
change	➔	FILL
clear	➔	ERASE
display	➔	CDUMP, DUMP, TYPE

Chapter 8

Mathematical Possibilities

"This sentence is false."
ancient (and wise) paradox

Quite a lot of any program is devoted to math of one sort or another. Just because you've been introduced to addition, subtraction, and other computations doesn't mean you know everything FORTH is capable of. In this chapter, you'll learn about the "other" mathematical possibilities FORTH allows.

Boolean Alley

The quotation at the beginning of this chapter is a paradox; it contradicts itself. Fortunately, such paradoxes aren't allowed in most programming languages.

Boolean arithmetic is the name given to computer truths and falsities. (This arithmetic is named for George Boole, the mathematician who first gave definition to the concept of true and false in math.)[1] Boolean arithmetic is sometimes referred to as "logical operations."

In most computers, there are two possible "Boolean values": false, which is represented by a zero, and true, which is represented by a one (often any nonzero number is treated as meaning "true").

A variable or memory location that contains a Boolean value is often said to be a "flag." If you see references to "flags" in the manual that accompanies your version of FORTH, it means that FORTH treats that value as being true or false.

The terms "flag" and "Boolean value" are used interchangeably in this book. It is also assumed that your version of FORTH, when it calculates a Boolean value, will output only a "0" for false or a "1" (for true).

Truth and Consequences

Why should FORTH need to know truths and falsehoods? The simple answer is that one of the necessities of programming is to be able to perform actions based upon certain conditions. Simply stated, the concept goes something like this:

**IF x IS TRUE, DO THIS-JOB,
BUT IF x IS FALSE, THEN DO THIS-OTHER-JOB.**

---

[1]George Boole. *An Investigation of the Laws of Thought.* Reprinted ed. New York: Dover Publications, 1964.

Old-time programmers call this process "conditional execution." That is, execution of a certain section of the program is contingent upon certain conditions being true.

Program-control structures (including conditional execution) are the subject of the next chapter. What you learn about the FORTH "logic" words in this chapter should help you understand how decisions are made in the conditional-control structures you'll learn about shortly.

──────────Testing, One, Two, Three──────────

Let's start by examining the concept of "tests." The basic idea is to take one element from the stack and test it against a predetermined number, or to take two values and compare them against one another.

You probably remember that there are many logical possibilities: is one number less than another, greater than another, or equal to another? The following is a list of the possibilities complete with the FORTH words that represent each test:

LOGICAL TEST	FORTH WORD
less than	$<$
greater than	$>$
equal to	$=$
less than or equal to	$\leq$
greater than or equal to	$\geq$
not equal to	$\neq$

You do each of these tests in the same manner. Put the two values you wish to test on the stack and execute the FORTH word. Thus,

$$6\ 9\ <$$

would test to see if the second number on the stack (6) is less than the top number on the stack (9). Since it is, FORTH leaves a value of 1 on the stack to indicate that it has encountered a truth and removes the "6" and "9."

The following is a summary of the three basic operations:

$$X\ Y\ < \quad \rightarrow \quad \text{is X less than Y?}$$
$$X\ Y\ > \quad \rightarrow \quad \text{is X greater than Y?}$$
$$X\ Y\ = \quad \rightarrow \quad \text{is X equal to Y?}$$

Now for some more operations, this time comparing one number against a predetermined value, consider the following:

LOGICAL TEST	FORTH WORD
greater than 0	0>
less than 0	0<
equal to 0	0=

NOTE: some versions of FORTH do not include the {0>} word. You can easily create it by typing

$$: \ 0> \ 0 \ > \ ;$$

In each of the above tests, you place one number on the stack, then execute the FORTH word for the test. Thus,

$$5 \ 0 >$$

tests to see if 5 is greater than 0 (it is, so a 1 is left on the stack and the 5 is removed).

If you're making a long calculation and then want to use the result to determine what section of the program to execute next, these "zero tests" become valuable indeed. By the way, you should notice one thing about the FORTH word {0=}. This really tests to see if a flag or value is false (that is, zero). This is a handy logical operation, because it effectively reverses the flag. (For computer types, that means that {0=} is similar to the logical equivalent of the "NOT" function. Unfortunately, most versions of FORTH test only a flag and do not perform a true "bitwise" logical NOT. Thus, the uses for this word are severely restricted.)

Shorthand Arithmetic

The truth test is one form of advanced arithmetic functions you'll want to use within FORTH. Another is what you might call "shorthand" arithmetic.

Two normal computer operations are "increment" and "decrement." These two terms really mean to "add 1" and "subtract 1," respectively. In FORTH, they add 1 or subtract 1 from the value on top of the stack.

{1+} increments the stack value by 1
{1-} decrements the stack value by 1

Some versions of FORTH also have words that add, subtract, multiply, or divide the stack by 2. As you would expect, these words look like the following:

{2+} increments the stack value by 2
{2-} decrements the stack value by 2
{2x} multiplies the stack value by 2
{2/} divides the stack value by 2

These shorthand operations are fine, but what if you want to add a number other than 1 or 2? If you want to add a specific number to a value stored in memory, you have to specify a sequence of execution something like the following:

VARIABLENAME @ VALUETOADD + VARIABLENAME !

If you have to do this often, you might find yourself doing a lot of typing. Also, you'll note that FORTH makes this a two-step operation when it really should be one step — this will slow things down slightly. Some versions of FORTH have a way of reducing this typing to

VALUETOADD VARIABLENAME +!

The more general form is

VALUE ADDRESS +!

FORTH adds the value to the number stored at the address specified and restores it at that location.

─────────────────── **Modern Times** ───────────────────

Since arithmetic in FORTH uses only integers, FORTH doesn't keep track of numbers to the right of the decimal point (usually referred to as "fixed-point" arithmetic). The limitation of integer-only arithmetic is no major problem if all you wish to do is add and subtract numbers (you can simply do all calculations without the decimal point and add it later when you display results). Say you want to add 32.45 and 27.

```
Mythical FORTH Version 1.1

Ok

32.45<CR>Ok

27.00<CR>Ok

D+<CR>Ok

<# # # ASCII . HOLD #s #> TYPE<CR>59.45Ok
```

For the moment, don't worry if you don't recognize much of the last line of coding above. It is simply a way of formatting double numbers with two digits to the left of the decimal place.

If we express this in other words, you could define a word that we'll call {ADDFIXEDPOINT} like the following:

: ADDFIXEDPOINT D+ <# # # ASCII . HOLD #s #> TYPE ;

↑

**this assumes that you are calculating with
two digits to left of the decimal point**

This new word required two double numbers on the top of the stack for addition. This is not an "intelligent" routine, because both values on the stack must have the same number of digits (that is, you must pad at least one with zeros if they are unequal in length, and you must predefine the number of digits to the left of the decimal place). Nevertheless, this simple routine should convince you that noninteger addition, multiplication, and subtraction are possible without much more knowledge than you already have accumulated.

Division with noninteger calculations is more difficult, however. With division the above routine won't work. Instead, you'll need to have separate small routines to work both the quotient and remainder in the operation.

{MOD} is an operation that divides the second number on the stack by the top one, and leaves the remainder as the only result on the stack.

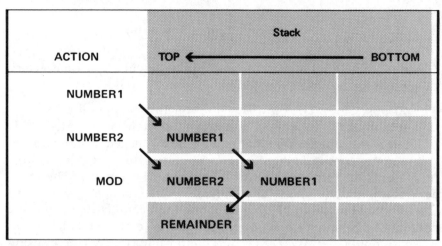

Notice that this operation differs from the {/} function only in that {/} leaves the quotient on the stack instead of the remainder.

A word or two concerning the remainder is necessary. Here's an example to illustrate.

14 divided by 6
quotient = 2
remainder = 2

If you're not familiar with the long division notation, the above example may surprise you. Long division works like the following:

$$
\begin{array}{r}
2 \\
6\,\overline{)\,1\,4} \\
\underline{1\,2}\quad(\text{2 times 6}) \\
2
\end{array}
$$

If you continued the long division, you would come up with the value you might have expected (2.3333). Modulo arithmetic (whence the FORTH word {MOD} derives) forces you to convert the remainder into the decimal value. To do so, you use a routine that works just like long division: add a zero to the right of the 2 (that is, multiply by 10) and divide by 6 again.

```
          2 . 3
    6  )  1 4 . 0
          1 2
          ―――
           2   0
           1   8    ( 3 times 6 )
           ―――
               2
```

Obviously, you do this same series of operations as often as necessary to achieve the precision you desire.

The purpose of this book is not to bog you down in complexities. For that reason, we'll leave the discussion of modulo arithmetic at this point. It was brought up so that you would not be led into the trap of thinking that noninteger (that is, fixed-point) arithmetic is impossible in FORTH, or that you can do it in the same manner as the other common math functions. There are several diabolical shortcuts to floating-point math with FORTH, but they fall completely outside the context of a beginner's book on the subject. A forthcoming book will present a number of advanced programming hints that will make using FORTH for floating-point arithmetic as easy as it is in other languages.

The Results Are In

Those of you with "math anxieties" shouldn't have been lost in this chapter. But just in case you're still shaking and need a refresher course on what was introduced in this chapter, the following is what you should have learned:

• Boolean values (or flags) are the computer's way of keeping track of truths or falsehoods. Generally, a value of zero represents false, and a value of one represents true.

• Conditional execution (coming up in the next chapter) is one reason you need true and false values.

• Several comparison tests are possible, all of which result in a true or false value being placed on the top of the stack.

$<$	**less than**
$>$	**greater than**
$=$	**equal to**

0>	**greater than zero**
0<	**less than zero**
0=	**equal to zero**

- Some shorthand addition math routines were introduced.

1+	**increment**
1-	**decrement**
2+	**increment by two**
2-	**decrement by two**
+!	**add a value to a value stored in memory**

- Fixed-point numbers were introduced, as well as a simple routine for addition, subtraction, and multiplication. Modulo math, used for noninteger division, was briefly discussed, along with a new word, {MOD}.

Chapter 9

Control Structures

"You Can't Get There from Here"
Ogden Nash, poem title

So far, what you've learned about FORTH makes it no more sophisticated than a memory calculator for which you can design the calculations you desire. If it is to be considered a language, it must have a way to control the flow of information. In this chapter, you'll learn how to make FORTH repeat operations and execute words only on specific conditions and how to manipulate the sequence in which instructions are executed.

―――――――――――――――――――――――――**I Do**―――――――――――――――――――

Perhaps the simplest control structure you can create is one that repeats an operation several times.

In FORTH, you control repetition by using the words {DO} and {LOOP} within a colon definition. Every word between these two special ones will repeat the number of times you specify. Actually, {DO} and {LOOP} form what is called an "indexed loop." That means that you control the number from which the loop starts counting and the number at which it stops counting, and you can use the current value of the loop for calculations.

Consider an example. Say that you are playing baseball. One of the key elements of that game is that you have to keep track of the outs to know when an inning (or half of an inning) is over. You start with no outs (that is, 0) and add 1 each time an out occurs. What happens between outs is execution of some sort.

{DO} and {LOOP} work similarly to our hypothetical baseball game. You can tell FORTH to start counting at 1 and count up to 3, and execute something between the counts.

: WORD 4 1 DO SOMETHING LOOP ;

Remember, {DO} loops can be used only in definitions; you cannot execute {DO} directly. The above example defines a word called {WORD}, which counts from 1 to 3. The general form in which you use {DO} and {LOOP} is

FINALVALUE+1 STARTVALUE DO words LOOP

In other words, the top value on the stack should be the starting value from which to count, with the final value plus one being the second number on the stack. You may have any number of words in between the {DO} and the {LOOP}, all of which will be executed for every value counted (in other words, counting from 1 to 3 will execute that group of words three times).

You don't have to specify the start and end values within the colon definition. One nice thing about FORTH is that as long as you keep track of where all the numbers are going to and coming from, you can pass values between words. Make sure you understand this last part. If you wanted to count from 1 to 5 and then later count from 2 to 10, you could type the following sequence:

```
Mythical FORTH Version 1.1

Ok

: AROUND DO I . LOOP ;<CR>Ok

6 1 AROUND<CR>1 2 3 4 5 Ok

11 2 AROUND<CR>2 3 4 5 6 7 8 9 10 Ok
```

In the above example, a new word, {I}, was introduced. This word puts the current "count" on the top of the stack. Thus, the sequence {I.} in the above example retrieves the count and displays it. Notice, by the way, that the numbers used for the beginning and ending counts for {AROUND} could have been calculated by another word or routine and left on the stack instead.

Use of an "index pointer" ({I} in most versions of FORTH) adds a great deal of flexibility to the concept of repeated loops. Remember, the index pointer puts the current count on the top of the stack, and the count could be used for calculations.

Suppose you wanted to calculate the squares of the numbers from 1 to 10. You could do this by defining a word like the following:

```
Mythical FORTH Version 1.1
Ok
: SQUARES DO I DUP * . LOOP ;<CR> Ok
11 1 SQUARES <CR>1 4 9 16 25 36 49 64 81
100 Ok
```

For each loop in the above example, what happens within FORTH is

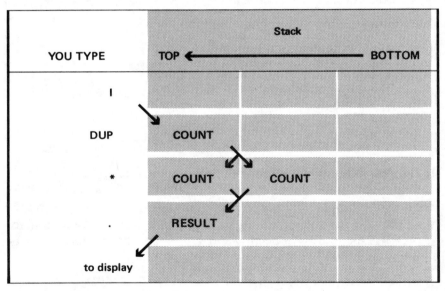

Notice how there is nothing on the stack at the beginning or end of the process. This is intentional. This particular routine doesn't have any effect on any others we may execute after it. Thus, it leaves the stack unmodified.

It is fine to develop routines that do change the stack, either by taking values off the stack or adding values to it. If you do this, however, be forewarned that you must pay particular attention to the sequence of words you execute. If you program haphazardly or ignore what's on the stack, you're likely to develop programs that don't function correctly, or don't function at all.

The Adjustable Loop

A second form of the {DO} loop operates in exactly the same fashion as that described above, except that you can tell FORTH to count by a number other than 1.

The general form of this second type of loop is

DO words INCREMENT +LOOP

Again, this loop can be used only within colon definitions.

You'll notice that the primary difference between this "adjustable" loop and the one described earlier is that you tell FORTH what number to count by (INCREMENT). You do not type "INCREMENT." Instead, you type the value you wish to increment the loop by. Depending on your version of FORTH, you can even count backward by specifying a negative number.

Mythical FORTH Version 1.1

Ok

: COUNTDOWN DO I . −1 +LOOP ;<CR> Ok

0 10 COUNTDOWN<CR> 10 9 8 7 6 5 4 3 2 1 Ok

To count backward you must specify a negative increment and make sure the two values you pass to the loop are suitable for counting backward.

────────────────────── **The Big {IF}**──────────────────────

Conditional execution has come up before and now it's time to learn how to use it. Perhaps you're like the author of this book and have said to yourself something like, "If I win the Pulitzer Prize, I'll vacation in Rio this year." That is conditional execution.

Conditional execution with FORTH is stated in a manner similar to the way you pondered the Pulitzer above.

IF true ➤ EXECUTION TAKES PLACE

You'll remember that in the last chapter you learned about Boolean values (TRUE/FALSE). To use conditional execution within FORTH, you leave a Boolean value on the stack and then execute the following general sequence of instructions:

IF words THEN
or
IF words ENDIF (depends upon version)

If the Boolean value was "true," execution of the words will take place; if the Boolean value was not "true," execution of the words will not take place. The conditional execution stops after the FORTH word {THEN} has been executed. Just like {DO}, {IF} can be used only within colon definitions.

That's easy enough, but have you ever said something like, "If I win the Pulitzer Prize, I'll vacation in Rio this year; but if I don't, I'll kill myself"? You'll note that two things can be executed: either buying a plane ticket to Rio (if the condition is true) or killing yourself (if the condition is false).

In FORTH, this "dual conditional" takes the form of:

IF words1 ELSE words2 THEN
or
IF words1 ELSE words2 ENDIF (depends upon version)

{Words1} would execute if the value on the top of the stack was "true," while {words2} would execute if the top stack value was "false." In other words, no matter what Boolean value is encountered, some additional instructions are followed.

You may embed {IF} statements within {IF} statements, if you wish. In other words, {IF} can be one of the words that executes when a condition is met.

IF IF words ELSE words THEN ELSE words THEN

is a valid FORTH structure. Remember, however, that there must be a Boolean value on the top of the stack for each {IF} encountered.

Programmers used to other languages (for example, BASIC, Pascal, and so on) might not be used to this horizontal representation of conditional execution, as it is extremely difficult to see embedded conditions. Another way to look at the general structure of {IF} is

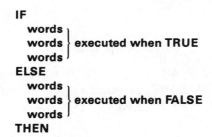

An embedded {IF} construction would look like the following:

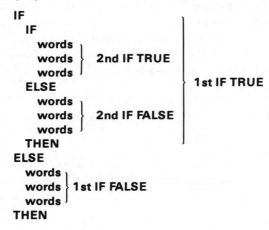

The {IF} functions give you the ability to add "thinking" to your FORTH program. All the FORTH words you've learned so far execute immediately. {IF} is the first that controls whether other words will execute. Using {IF} allows you to put intelligence into your program to determine which set of instructions should be used.

Don't jump to any conclusions about this "intelligence," however. Your computer can't really think, but the {IF} function does add an enormous flexibility to your programming — so much, in fact, that you'll be able to create complex "logic paths" for individual tasks you assign the computer.

Let Me {BEGIN} {AGAIN}

Yet another conditional construct in FORTH programming is that of the {BEGIN} function. {BEGIN} has three common forms.

The first {BEGIN} construct is actually an unconditional loop (that is, it will be repeated indefinitely). Newcomers to FORTH might be surprised to see a language with the ability to create a built-in "endless loop."

BEGIN words AGAIN

In the above example, all of the FORTH words that appear between {BEGIN} and {AGAIN} will be repeated — in sequence — essentially forever. {BEGIN} must be used within colon definitions; it cannot execute directly.

To keep the above loop from going on indefinitely, you should add an option that lets you terminate execution. You can choose one of two common FORTH words: {BYE} returns you to the operating-system level and {COLD} restarts FORTH. In addition, you can use the words {WARM}, {QUIT}, {ABORT}, or {EXIT} to terminate execution — check your FORTH manual to see how to use each.

A second {BEGIN} construct is to repeat the series of instructions until a certain condition has been met. The general form for this is

BEGIN words flag UNTIL

You don't type the word {flag}, but instead leave a flag on the stack. If the flag (Boolean value, remember?) is "true," the loop will repeat.

The last way to use {BEGIN} is to have an "exit test" in the middle of the loop, a construct that Pascal and other languages don't have.

BEGIN words flag WHILE (words) REPEAT

The "(words)" in the above example indicates that you can place the test for falsehood anywhere within the loop, as opposed to the {BEGIN} - {UNTIL} construct, which requires that the test of the flag occur at the end of the sequence of words constituting the loop. As before, you don't type {flag}; instead, you leave a flag on the stack just prior to executing the {WHILE} statement.

Other Control Structures

You can combine several of the control structures presented here to make new, more complex ones.

Some versions of FORTH have invented some of these new structures for you. One common extension of the FORTH language involves the {CASE} statement, an imitation of the Pascal statement of the same name. Instead of testing for true or false, the {CASE} function allows you to define procedures based upon the value encountered on the stack. In other words, if FORTH found a "5" on the stack it would do one thing, "6" would make it do another, and so on. This is a particularly powerful function, as it allows you to define "multiple branching" within your program. If your version of FORTH supports {CASE} statements, you would do well to thoroughly investigate its use. If such a statement doesn't exist in your FORTH, you could program one yourself (see Appendix F for an example).

Out of Control

Don't underestimate the capabilities of the control structures presented in this chapter. They will constitute the bulk of the structure of your FORTH programs. Following is a quick summary of the words you learned in this chapter and their functions

● **STOP#+1 START# {DO} words {LOOP}** This construct allows you to repeat a sequence of words a specified number of times. The loop counts in increments of 1.

● **STOP+#1 START# {DO} words value {+LOOP}**   This construct allows you to repeat a sequence of words while "counting" in increments of other than 1.

● **{I}**   Places the current "count" on the top of the stack during execution of a loop.

● **flag {IF} words {THEN}**   This sequence executes the words specified if, and only if, the flag is true.

● **flag {IF} words {ELSE} words {THEN}**   One set of words will execute if the flag is true, while another sequence of words executes if the flag is false.

● **{BEGIN} words {AGAIN}**   The words {BEGIN} and {AGAIN} will repeat indefinitely.

● **{BEGIN} words flag {UNTIL}**   The words between {BEGIN} and {UNTIL} execute until the flag value left on the stack at the end of the sequence of words is true.

● **{BEGIN} words flag {WHILE} words {REPEAT}**   The sequence of words executes until the value of the flag is false.

Chapter 10

Input
And Output

"Nowhere to go but out, nowhere to come but back."
Benjamin Franklin King, The Pessimist

FORTH wouldn't be very useful if it wasn't able to "talk to" all the components of your computer. This chapter will teach you the basic input and output routines built into standard FORTH, with primary emphasis on use of your mass-storage device, the disk.

────────────── Texting, One, Two, Three ──────────────

You've already been introduced to several FORTH words that perform rudimentary input and output. To jog your memory, these words are

.	display top stack element
EMIT	display one ASCII byte
KEY	input one character

As you may have suspected, there are other console input and output routines in FORTH. Using {EMIT} would be a cumbersome method of displaying a large string of characters, especially if these characters never changed. In BASIC, you can output a predefined sequence of statements by using a PRINT statement.

PRINT "Now is the time for all . . ."

This would display "Now is the time for all . . ." on the console screen, for instance. FORTH has a function that is the equivalent of BASIC's PRINT statement.

." Now is the time for all . . ."

The FORTH word {."} indicates that the string of characters up to the next set of quotation marks is to be literally displayed on the console. Remember that all input to FORTH must be separated by spaces, so you must leave a space after {."} before starting the text you want displayed, but not before the terminating quotation mark.

If there's a way to output a long sequence of characters, it stands to reason that there should be a way to input a long sequence of characters, as well. There is.

You usually use the FORTH word {EXPECT} to get programs to request a long string of characters from users. To use {EXPECT}, you must leave an address and a value on the stack. The address indicates where in memory you want FORTH to begin saving the typed characters, while the value represents the number of characters it should expect.

A common convention in data entry is to use the carriage return key (an ASCII value of 13) to terminate the entry of information, and {EXPECT} will stop storing characters you type at the terminal when it detects a carriage return or when it receives the total number of characters it expects, whichever comes first.

16000 13 EXPECT

This would store 13 characters beginning at memory location 16000 (decimal). To display the characters you stored using {EXPECT}, you could use the following:

ADDRESS NUMBEROFCHARACTERS TYPE

—————————————— **Terminal Vocabulary** ——————————————

Terminals today generally have sophisticated displays. If you know the right sequence of values, you can erase everything from the screen simultaneously, move the cursor at random, create inverse video characters, and so on.

Unfortunately, many versions of FORTH don't have any built-in words to accomplish these desirable functions. At a minimum, you need to have the following functions available:

- Clear the screen

- Move the cursor to any position

- Produce inverse (or enhanced) video

- Suspend inverse (or enhanced) video.

If your version of FORTH doesn't have these building blocks, then you may build them yourself. On a Vector Graphic computer, for instance, you would define these four functions like the following:

```
: CLEAR 4 EMIT ;
: GOTO-XY 27 EMIT EMIT EMIT ;
```
                    ↓   ↓
            assumes values on the stack

```
: BRIGHT 20 EMIT ;
: DIM 20 EMIT ;
```

If you're not sure how your console works or how to make it do these four things, it would be a good thing to visit your local computer club or computer store and find out, as these four added functions can make your FORTH programs much more efficient and "cleaner looking."

Ports — All Ashore Who's Going Ashore

Most microcomputers can have as many as 256 input/output ports. The most frequent use of these ports is to hook peripherals (such as a printer) to computers, although sometimes they are used internally by computers for special tasks.

(WARNING: If you're not sure what ports are used on your computer for what purposes, make sure that you are using a copy of your usual FORTH diskette and have nothing in memory that you cannot duplicate quickly. The reason for this is that, on some computers, probing around among the I/O ports can cause anything—from erasure of portions of the disk to completely restarting the machine. It would be unusual for you to cause something to happen, but since it is possible, you should be prepared for the worst.)

Getting characters to and from the I/O ports works the same as with memory.

P@ ← gets a character from a port
P! ← sends a character to a port

Instead of a memory address needing to be on the stack, port operations require the port address to be there (it is usually in the range of 0 to 255). To get a character from I/O port 4, you would type

4 P@

To send a carriage-return character to a port, you would type

13 4 P!

Not all versions of FORTH will have port I/O operations available, as the design of some computers is such that there are no ports, per se. Many of the computers that do not utilize I/O ports instead use a memory location to substitute for the port (as in "memory-mapped I/O"). For these computers, you might be able to create the following FORTH words (so that your programs will remain consistent no matter what machine they run on):

: P! address C! ;
:P@ address C@ ;

———— Disk Could Be The Start of Something Big ————

Most microcomputers are limited in the amount of information they can address at one time (usually 64K bytes). Even with more memory (as in the case of the 256K-equipped computers now being introduced) it often turns out that FORTH and other languages cannot easily use the additional memory.

One solution to the dilemma of having only a fixed amount of memory available at one time is called "virtual memory," in which a disk drive or tape drive substitutes for a portion of memory. Users of systems that feature virtual memory are often unaware that pieces of memory are constantly being loaded from or saved onto a diskette. Disk drives are available on most FORTH systems and make an almost unlimited amount of storage space available, albeit not all at the same time. In a limited way, FORTH is a virtual-memory system.

FORTH does not necessarily use the space on a diskette in the same manner as a disk-operating system does. Most operating systems deal with the disk in small "chunks."

FORTH accesses the disk in 1K-byte (1024-character) chunks, regardless of how the standard operating system for your computer stores and retrieves information. A small but growing number of FORTH implementations are abandoning the 1K-byte "block" concept, although those that do can be classified only as derivatives of FORTH.

In short, every time FORTH places information on the disk, it does so 1024 characters at a time, and every time FORTH gets information from the disk, it retrieves 1024 characters at a time.

Information is passed between FORTH and the disk drives via "buffers." A buffer is just an area of memory reserved for temporary storage of information. A complete 1024-character set of information is called a "block" in FORTH terminology. Thus, to save information to a diskette, you move a block of characters to the disk buffer and tell FORTH to save it.

Retrieving information works in a similar manner. You ask FORTH to get a block, which is copied from the specified area on the diskette to the temporary buffer, from which you can then retrieve or use the information in any manner you wish.

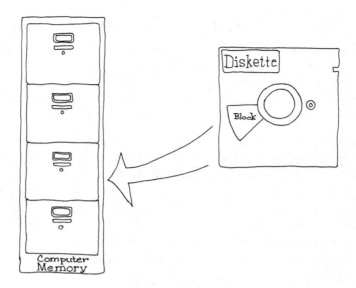

Blocks are stored on the disk consecutively and are numbered (beginning at zero) sequentially. This means that the very first 1024 characters of information on a diskette are known as block number zero, the second group as block number one, and so forth.

Each block is usually considered to comprise further divisions. Traditionally blocks are divided into 16 lines of 64 characters each. Standard FORTH has no direct way of manipulating these subdivisions, although an editing program that accompanies the language usually provides this ability.

Earlier it was mentioned in passing that you can change the error messages in FORTH. The reason you can is that they are stored on your FORTH diskette. Each version of FORTH may be a bit different, but generally the very first available blocks are reserved for error messages. In most versions of FORTH, two blocks are used for error messages. You should probably reserve two more blocks (two and three) for error messages you invent as you program.

Each error message can be as many as 64 characters long, and each block can contain as many as 16 error messages. If these numbers sound familiar, you're right, they're the subdivisions mentioned earlier in this chapter (a few paragraphs ago).

The first error message in the first block is error message number 1. The second is error message number 2, and so on. One oddity is that the first line in a FORTH block is usually reserved for a "comment" or identification, so there is no such thing as error message 0 or error message 16. The numbering scheme continues across blocks. The first line of the second block is error message number 17, the first line of the third block is error message number 33, and so on.

```
{ Sample Screen of FORTH Error Messages }

SCR # 0

   0    FORTH Copyright (c) 1981  The Software Works, Inc.

   1    The stack is empty.

   2    The dictionary is full.

   3    has incorrect address mode.

   4    isn't unique.

   5    An obscure error of the fifth kind has occurred.

   6    Illegal block number requested.

   7

   8

   9

  10

  11

  12    CP/M Error — Seek to unwritten extent.

  13    CP/M Error — Directory overflow.

  14    CP/M Error — Seek past physical end of disk.

  15    Software Works FORTH for CP/M 2.X  Rev-2

  Ok
```

When FORTH encounters an error, a number is associated with that error. This number tells FORTH where to find the error message associated with it, as described in the previous paragraph.

You needn't wait for FORTH to detect an error to display an error message. You can display any of the FORTH messages at any time by placing the number of the one you wish displayed on the top of the stack and then typing the word {MESSAGE}.

CP/M systems using FORTH that do not use standard CP/M files will not have error messages associated with block number 0. The reason for this is that the CP/M system and file directory are located on the disk in the exact locations of the first few blocks. Most CP/M FORTHs start the error messages with block number 4.

I/O You an Explanation

It's time to deal with the many disk functions provided in FORTH. To load a disk block into the temporary buffer, you place the number of the block you wish to load and then type the word {BLOCK}. When the information has been copied to the buffer, the top element of the stack will be the memory address of the start of the buffer.

Displaying the information in block number 79 would, therefore, be as simple as typing the following:

79 BLOCK 1024 TYPE

An annotated version of the above might be

79	(block number to retrieve)
BLOCK	(load the block into buffer)
	(leaves address of start of)
	(block on stack)
1024	(number of characters to)
	(display)
TYPE	(display the block)

You may change anything in the buffer using other FORTH functions. After you've done so, you'll want to save those changes back to the diskette. To do so, you first type the FORTH word {UPDATE}. {UPDATE} makes the buffer "dirty" — a programmer's term to mean that you have changed the information in the buffer.

Unlike many other words, {UPDATE} does not require a number on the stack; it assumes that the last block you accessed is the one you want to save. FORTH automatically keeps track of the last block you accessed. {UPDATE} does not actually save the changes you made — it only marks the buffer as needing "updating." You use the FORTH word {SAVE-BUFFERS} to actually save the information.

In fact, you can find out the number of the last block you accessed by using the FORTH word {BLK}. Typing {BLK @} will place a number on the top of the stack that equals the last block number you retrieved.

This is not to imply that you can't manipulate more than one block at once. The number of buffers you have available in memory varies among versions of FORTH, but usually there are at least two or three.

Each time you copy information from the diskette to the buffers, FORTH assigns this new information an unused buffer, assuming there's one left. If you already have something in all the buffers, FORTH automatically writes the information in the first buffer you accessed (assuming that there were changes, that is, you marked the block using {UPDATE}) back to disk and uses that emptied space to place the information it has been asked to retrieve.

To save all buffers in use back to disk at once, you employ the {SAVE-BUFFERS} command. All updated blocks will be saved onto disk.

To clear the buffers without saving the information in them, you use a command named {EMPTY-BUFFERS}.

There is much, much more to disk I/O, but it belongs in the context of the FORTH editor and the creation, saving, and retrieval of programs, which is the subject of the next chapter.

—————I/O, I/O, It's Off to Work You Go—————

You encountered a lot of information in this chapter. These main points should now seem familiar:

• To display a long string of unchanging characters on your display you use the word {."}.

• To input a long string of characters to FORTH you use the word {EXPECT}.

• Four terminal functions are essential to good programming, although they may not be present in your version of FORTH. If your FORTH doesn't have them, you'll want to create the following words:

CLEAR   GOTO-XY   BRIGHT   DIM

• FORTH stores information on the diskette in "blocks" of 1024 characters, numbered sequentially. Information passes between FORTH and the diskette via buffers.

• Error messages are stored in the first available disk blocks and are numbered sequentially across blocks.

• You also learned some basic disk I/O operations, including

BLOCK	load a block to buffer
UPDATE	save a block from buffer
BLK	places last block # on stack
SAVE-BUFFERS	saves all buffers to disk (FLUSH in older systems)
EMPTY-BUFFERS	clears all buffers in memory

Chapter II

Programming
In FORTH

"Man ever had, and ever will have,
leave to coin new words well suited to the age."
Horace, Ars Poetica

If you were wondering if all the information in this book would ever coagulate into a coherent whole, this is the chapter for you. To be useful, any computer language must allow programmers to shape their instructions and make them permanent. Although you've already experimented with pieces of what FORTH can do, this chapter should begin to make you feel that the whole is greater than the sum of its parts.

Screening FORTH

In the last chapter you learned that FORTH stores information on diskettes in blocks of 1024 characters and that each block consists of 16 lines of 64 characters each.

Those numbers are not coincidences. Most of the earliest display terminals of microcomputer systems featured 16 lines of 64 characters each. The reason for this is that 16 multiplied by 64 just happens to equal 1024, a magic number in computing, as it happens to be 2 to the power of 10. (Remember, computers tend to do everything in binary; thus, powers of 2 make a lot of sense.)

It should come as no surprise that FORTH users often refer to information on diskettes as "screens." Sometimes the term "page" is substituted for screen, but the two words mean the same thing, and both refer to the basic block concept described earlier.

Since a screen of information uses the entire area of most computer displays, editors were developed to facilitate the creation and alteration of an entire disk block of information. So far, you haven't learned how to save the work you program into FORTH. You don't know how because you have yet to learn about the editor that accompanies your version of FORTH.

While all FORTH editors don't use the same commands, they are conceptually the same. You tell FORTH what screen you wish to edit. That screen is loaded into memory and/or placed on your display. You enter new material, make changes and deletions and then you save the screen back to disk.

What you usually enter on those screens is colon definitions. This is the permanent storage of your FORTH programming, sometimes called "source code" to indicate that it is the original source of instructions to the machine.

─────────────Screen Presumptions─────────────

FORTH makes some presumptions about the screens you save on disk. You needn't follow these assumptions if you don't want to, but since most of them make programming in FORTH much easier, it is a good idea to learn them.

FORTH programmers commonly use the first line of each screen for comments. Comments are descriptions of what is taking place and FORTH ignores them when compiling colon definitions. Comments in FORTH are defined as being all material within a set of parentheses. Again, since FORTH needs a space between distinct actions, leave a space after the left parenthesis and your comment:

> (This is a valid comment.)
> (This would not be a valid comment.)
> (This (is (a (valid (comment, too!)
> (But (this is) not.)

One of FORTH's commands is {INDEX}. By putting the first and last screen numbers you wish to index on the stack and typing {INDEX}, you'll see the first line of each of the screens that is in the range you specify:

```
Mythical FORTH Version 1.1

Ok

1 10 INDEX<CR>


 1   ( FORTH error messages )

 2   ( more FORTH error messages )

 3   ( reserved )

 4   ( reserved )

 5   ( Terminal Definitions )

 6   ( Printer Definitions )

 7

 8

 9   ( MYPROGRAM start )

10   ( MYPROGRAM page two )Ok
```

Notice in the above example that screens 7 and 8 appear not to have anything on them. The numbers which start each line, by the way, are supplied by FORTH; they do not appear in those screens. Notice also that everything that appears in the {INDEX} is a valid FORTH comment.

It is possible to put colon definitions on the first line of a screen, but such a practice would not necessarily indicate what else was on that screen.

You can see everything that appears in a disk block by using the command {LIST}. By placing the number of the screen you wish to look at on the top of the stack and then typing {LIST}, you'll get a complete list of that screen.

```
Mythical FORTH Version 1.1
Ok
89 LIST<CR>
SCR # 89
  0   ( PAGE 3 OF FIG-FORTH EDITOR          )
  1   : H                 ( HOLD LINE AT PAD )
  2      LINE PAD 1+ C/L DUP PAD C! CMOVE ;
  3
  4   : E          ( ERASE LINE-1 WITH BLANKS )
  5      LINE C/L BLANKS UPDATE ;
  6
  7   : S       ( SPREAD  MAKING LINE # BLANK )
  8      DUP 1 - ( LIMIT ) 0E ( 1ST MOVED )
  9         DO I LINE I 1+ -MOVE -1 +LOOP E ;
 10
 11   : D       ( DELETE LINE-1, BUT HOLD IT )
 12      DUP H 0F DUP ROT
 13         DO I 1+ LINE I -MOVE LOOP E ;
 14
 15   ⟶
```

If you take a close look at the above screen, you'll notice several things that haven't come up yet.

1. You may leave as many blanks between FORTH words as you desire (including carriage returns) without affecting the performance of programs. These extra blanks increase "readability" of a program.

2. Comments may appear at any point within a colon definition; they will not be compiled.

3. To use a word in a colon definition, it must already have been defined. Notice that line 9 makes use of a word defined in line 4, while line 12 makes use of a word defined in line 1. You'll learn about this "top-down" structure later.

4. All of the definitions presented are short (the longest shown consists of 13 FORTH words). If you find that you are writing colon definitions with more than 20 words in them, check carefully to make sure that each word has a unique function (that is, it doesn't try to do more than one task; this makes debugging easier).

5. Line 8 contains the characters "0E" and line 12 contains "0F." Programmers will recognize this as being hexadecimal notation. FORTH will happily work in any number base you desire (see the word {BASE} in Appendix B).

You'll also note several new FORTH words in the example on the previous page. Most of these will not be elaborated on here, as they are quite advanced.

The word {—>}, however, deserves some mention. The word {—>} means that the current page is linked to the next one (that is, the source code is continued on the next screen).

To get the definitions on screens compiled into FORTH, you place the starting screen number on the top of the stack and type the word {LOAD}.

23 LOAD

When FORTH gets to the end of screen number 23, if it hasn't encountered {—>}, it will stop loading at the end of that page. If it sees a {—>}, FORTH will continue by loading the next screen, as well. Obviously, this can continue for as many screens as you desire.

The word {—>} is not in a colon definition. You can intermix direct commands to FORTH with colon definitions in your screens. It would be possible, for instance, to clear the screen and present a user message while loading colon definitions. An example of such a screen might be something like the following:

```
Mythical FORTH Version 1.1

Ok

20 LIST <CR>

SCR #20

    0    ( START OF MY WONDERFUL PROGRAM )

    1    CLEAR            ( CLEAR THE SCREEN )

    2    CR CR CR CR      ( GO DOWN FOUR LINES )  ←—  direct
                                                       commands
    3    ." ONE MOMENT WHILE I LOAD UP . . . "

    4

    5    : TEXT HERE C/L 1+ BLANKS WORD

    6          HERE PAD C/L 1+ CMOVE ;  ←————————  colon
                                                    definitions
    7

    8    : LINE DUP FFF0 AND 17 ?ERROR

    9          SCR @ (LINE) DROP ;

   10

   11  →    ←————————————————————————————  keep
                                             loading
   12

   13

   14

   15

Ok
```

113

To stop the loading and compiling of a program, you can also use the word {;S}. It isn't always necessary, but it is wise to use it anyway to prevent accidents. Whenever you use {;S}, all loading of information from the disk block stops. Thus, any colon definition or information following a {;S} will not load. Also, {;S} is an "immediate" word; therefore, it is not usually used *within* a colon definition.

Programming with the Top Down

Once you've learned the command structure of the editor that comes with your version of FORTH, you know enough to begin programming in FORTH.

FORTH is a language well suited to "top-down" programming. While a few programming purists will object to the definition, let's define top-down programming as the practice of first defining the objective, then working backward until you know exactly what modules are needed to achieve it.

If you were to design a sports car using the top-down method, you'd first define what a sports car is.

- Fast

- Fun

- Small

- Good handling

- Sexy design.

Now, none of the above items tells exactly how to build the car, so you'll need to continue refining your objectives. Consider the term "fast," for instance.

- Efficient motor

- Lots of torque

- Low weight

- High-performance tires

- Fuel injection implied

- Aerodynamic design implied.

You still haven't "designed" your car, though. You could take the term "reduce weight" and break it into further components.

- Use aluminum in doors, hood

- Eliminate nonfunctional items

- Use plastic in interior

- Use special mix with plastic in windows.

You still haven't designed the car. Taking the aluminum in the doors and the hood section, you could now say

- Make doors in two pieces

- Make hood in one piece

- Use "breaks" in metal instead of support beams to provide strength.

You could go on almost indefinitely in this definition process. You'll eventually end up with a list of parts and a description of how those parts interlock to make the car.

Programming in FORTH works the same way. Let's assume that you wish to write a word processing program. The first task in top-down programming is to define what you think word processing implies:

- Insertion of material

- Ability to change material

- Deletion of material.

You could then further subdivide each of these definitions into subdefinitions. Eventually, you'll end up with the "bill of materials" (parts list) and a blueprint for how they program in FORTH; the rest of the process can take place on paper, in your brain, or wherever you prefer to store information.

Newcomers to programming often take the opposite approach. They say they want to write a word processing program and immediately sit down and begin writing and testing code. At best, such a program will grow haphazardly; at worst it won't work.

In working with FORTH you are working at a level extremely close to the "heart" of the computer when you begin programming. Other computer languages allow you to work at a much higher conceptual level from the beginning, but with FORTH you generally must start out by laying a solid foundation.

In a manner of speaking, you *write* programs in FORTH from the "bottom up," even though the design process takes place from the top down. This is not a contradiction. When you begin writing a program in FORTH, you are making the nails, a pile of miscellaneous wood, and some paint — later on, you get to build the house. It does you no good to build and paint the roof first, and if you're not working from a blueprint, you might find that the roof doesn't fit the house.

Other high-level languages give you bigger building blocks to work with. In BASIC and Pascal, for instance, *you* build your house using walls, floors, and support beams. The primary difference between FORTH and these other languages is that in FORTH *you* get to design the walls, floors, and support beams, whereas in BASIC and Pascal, they are already designed for you.

———————————Programming Review———————————

While this chapter was long on words, it is easy to summarize in a short space.

• You save colon definitions by saving them on screens (disk blocks).

• You indicate nonexecutable commentary by using parentheses to isolate the comments. Comments may appear anywhere, even within colon definitions; it is a standard practice to place a comment on the first line of every screen of information.

• You learned several FORTH words that apply specifically to the manipulation of screens including

INDEX	**displays first lines of several screens**
—>	**links screens**
LOAD	**loads a screen or series of linked screens**
;S	**stops the loading of screens**

• You also learned about top-down programming and its relationship to FORTH.

Chapter 12

And So: FORTH

" 'I shall sit here,' he said,
'on and off, for days and days.' "
Lewis Carroll, Alice's Adventures in Wonderland

Before you read the last words in this book and wander off to invent FORTH words of your own, some last observations seem in order.

Is It Worth It

Although it may seem like a long time ago, you had to learn to speak and understand English. At first, that language probably seemed remarkably inefficient and confusing. Most people say the same thing about FORTH when they first encounter it.

The question that comes to mind is: will FORTH be worth the effort? No one else can answer that question for you. But consider the advantages of FORTH.

First, FORTH is efficient. It takes up little memory space, especially when compared to other languages that evolved on large computer systems.

Second, programming in FORTH, while tough to understand at first, becomes simpler and simpler the more you use it. The reason for this is that you build blocks at the bottom of the pyramid when you first program in FORTH, but can concentrate later on the top levels instead of reinventing routines. You'll find that words you create for one program will find use in later programs, making you more efficient in the long run.

Third, FORTH programs seem more conducive to "tuning." In the bottom layer of FORTH programming, you deal with primitive functions. If you become a good FORTH programmer, you'll become more aware of the limitations of the machine you are working with and become more adept at working around the restrictions. FORTH is a language in which it is always possible to make your program faster, less error-prone, and more flexible. And when you do make changes to your FORTH programs, you'll find that you can make modifications faster and without having to change the entire program.

Fourth, FORTH is one of the few languages that offers exactly the same version for a number of different microprocessors. The "transporting" of a FORTH program between different computers is easy. In fact, at least one firm is working on a method by which blocks of FORTH screens and definitions can be exchanged between any two computers that can communicate with one another.

Last, FORTH is extensible. You can redefine the language any time you desire. If you don't think the word {!} is indicative of the operation it performs, nothing stops you from redefining by typing in a colon definition such as

: **STORE !** ;

If you redefined every FORTH word, your execution speed would slow down slightly, but compared to BASIC, FORTH has speed and space to spare. (Actually, if you go on to become an expert FORTH programmer, you'll learn a way to redefine the language without any loss in speed or efficiency.)

You make up your mind. FORTH may seem like gobbledygook to you now, but if you give it a chance, you just might grow to like it.

So What's Next

Assuming that you've decided to proceed with using FORTH, you'll eventually need far more information than you received from this book. Programming is not a simple chore, nor one that can be taken lightly.

Your first step on completing this book should be to grab your FORTH diskette and manual and begin experimenting. While your eventual goal may be to create complex programs, remember that one of FORTH's attributes is that it allows you to work with small "chunks" of a task at a time. Start with these tasks and use them to define bigger ones.

Once you're starting to feel at home with FORTH, you should read a book or two on structured programming, particularly one with an emphasis on top-down programming. There are more books on the subject than there's room for here, but two helpful ones are *Software Debugging for Microcomputers* and Dijkstra's *A Discipline of Programming*. Browse through some at your local technical bookstore and pick a structured-programming book that seems "comfortable" to you.

The third step in increasing your knowledge of FORTH is to read the manual that came with your FORTH as you would read a dictionary if you were trying to memorize it. Get every word into your vocabulary and practice it to keep it there. If you're proficient at assembly language, you might also want to get the source code for your computer from the FORTH Interest Group. Also, several useful books on FORTH have appeared including Byte Books' *Threaded Interpretive Languages* and Prentice Hall's *Starting FORTH*.

No one can tell you *exactly* how to program. Programming in FORTH is like a craft: an individual's skill and interpretation often have both functional and artistic results. What you can accomplish with FORTH is limited only by the amount of time you spend with the language and your imagination. If this book has made the process of learning about FORTH easier or has suggested an idea you hadn't considered before, its purpose has been served.

Appendices

A: Coding Sheet for FORTH Programming
B: FORTH-79 Standard—Glossary of Words
C: ASCII Character Codes
D: Suggested Alternatives to the FORTH Syntax
E: Error Messages
F: Some FORTH Extensions

Coding Sheet for FORTH Programming

Word: _____   Date: _____

Page: _____   Vocabulary: _____   Programmer: _____

Stack Upon Entry: _____ items

Upon Exit: _____ items

Top ⟵——————— STACK ⟵——————— Bottom

ACTION	1	2	3	4	5	6

——FORTH-79 Standard — Glossary of Words——

This appendix presents the required set of FORTH words that constitute the FORTH-79 Standard. The FORTH-79 Standard was first published in October 1980, and represents the FORTH community's attempt to create a universal definition of the language.

The words described here do not necessarily constitute the full complement of vocabulary your version of FORTH might contain. The Glossary is in ASCII sort sequence.

The following conventions are used throughout this glossary:

addr	a value representing a byte's address
byte	a value representing an 8-bit byte
char	a value representing a 7-bit ASCII code
flag	a Boolean value (0 = false, 1 = true)
n	a 16-bit signed integer
un	a 16-bit unsigned integer
d	a 32-bit signed double number
ud	a 32-bit unsigned double number
<NAME>	user-supplied name (used for variables, and so forth)
<TEXT>	user-supplied text

The shorthand method used to indicate stack parameters before and after execution of a word places the top of the stack at the right side of a line.

!   **n addr !**
Stores number at address specified.

**ud1 # ud2**
Generates the next ASCII character to be placed in an output string from an unsigned double number. The result stored on the stack is the quotient after division by the current base and is maintained for further processing. Used between <# and #>.

#>   **d # addr n**
Ends pictured numeric output conversion. The double number is dropped from the stack, replaced with an address and a number that represent the starting location and number of characters of the converted text, respectively.

#S   **ud #S 0 0**

Converts all digits of an unsigned double number, adding each to the pictured numeric output until the remainder is zero. If the number was initially 0, a single 0 is added to the output string. Used between <# and #>.

'   **' <NAME> addr**

Leaves the address of the named word on the stack.

*   **n1 n2 * n3**

Leaves the product of the two numbers on the stack.

*/   **n1 n2 n3 */ n4**

Multiplies the first and second number, divides the result by the third number, and leaves the quotient on the stack. The quotient is rounded toward zero. The intermediary result (after n1 * n2) is a double number, resulting in greater precision than n1 n2 * n3 /.

*/MOD   **n1 n2 n3 */MOD n4 n5**

Multiplies the first and second number, divides the result by the third number, and leaves the remainder as the fourth number and the quotient as the fifth. The intermediary result (after n1 * n2) is a double number. The remainder has the same sign as the first number.

(**(<TEXT>)**

All characters following this word up to and including the next right parenthesis are considered a comment and are ignored by FORTH.

+   **n1 n2 + n3**

Adds the first two single numbers together and leaves the result on the stack.

+LOOP   **n +LOOP**

Adds the signed number to the loop-index count and compares the total to the limit. If the loop-index count is less than the limit, execution is returned to the corresponding DO command. Loop control parameters are discarded when the loop is completed.

-   **n1 n2 - n3**

Subtracts the second single number from the first number and leaves the difference on the stack.

-TRAILING   **addr n1 -TRAILING addr n2**

Adjusts the character count of a text string beginning at the address specified to exclude all trailing blanks.

,   **n ,**

Allots two bytes in the dictionary for the word being defined and stores the number indicated there.

.   **n .**

Displays the number indicated in the current numeric base with a single blank after the result. A negative sign is displayed only if the number is less than zero.

."   **."<TEXT>"**

Displays the user-supplied text on the current output device. The FORTH-79 Standard requires that at least 127 characters be allowed in the user-supplied text, although some versions allow more.

:   **: <TEXT>**

Used to begin a colon definition (that is, compilation). User-supplied text must be valid FORTH words or instructions.

;

Used to end a colon definition (see above).

/   **n1 n2 / n3**

Divides the first number by the second and leaves the quotient on the stack. The quotient is rounded toward zero.

/MOD   **n1 n2 /MOD n3 n4**

Divides the first number by the second and leaves the remainder as the third number and the quotient as the fourth. The remainder has the same sign as the first number.

0<   **n 0< flag**

Leaves a "true" flag if the number is less than zero —otherwise "false."

0=   **n 0= flag**

Leaves a "true" if the number is zero — otherwise "false."

0>   **n 0> flag**

Leaves a "true" if the number is greater than zero —otherwise "false."

1+   **n 1+ n+1**

Increments the number by one.

1-   **n 1- n-1**

Decrements the number by one.

2+   **n 2+ n+2**

Increments the number by two.

2-   **n 2- n-2**
Decrements the number by two.

79-STANDARD   **79-STANDARD**
Assures that a FORTH-79 Standard vocabulary is available for use.

<   **n1 n2 < flag**
Leaves a "true" if the first number is less than the second — otherwise "false."

<#   **<# # #S HOLD SIGN #>**
Used to initialize a pictured numeric output for a double-number into an ASCII character string stored in left-to-right order.

=   **n1 n2 = flag**
Leaves a "true" if the first numbers equals the second — otherwise "false."

>   **n1 n2 > flag**
Leaves a "true" if the first number is greater than the second — otherwise "false."

>IN   **>IN addr**
Leaves the address of a variable on the stack that contains the present character offset within an input stream.

>R   **n >R**
Places the number specified on the return stack. Every >R should be balanced by an R> in the same control-structure nesting level of a colon definition.

?   **addr ?**
Displays the number stored at the address.

?DUP   **n ?DUP n (n)**
Duplicates the number indicated if it is not equal to zero. Otherwise, the stack is unchanged.

@   **addr @ n or <NAME> @ n**
Leaves the number stored at the address specified on the stack.

ABORT   **ABORT**
Clears all stacks and returns control to the terminal in the execution mode.

ABS   **n1 ABS n2**
Leaves the absolute value of a number on the stack.

ALLOT   **n ALLOT**
Adds the number of bytes specified to the parameter field of the most recently defined word.

AND   **n1 n2 AND n3**
Leaves the logical "AND" of the first two numbers on the stack. The "AND" operation is performed bit by bit.

BASE   **BASE addr**
Leaves the address of a variable that contains the current numeric base on the stack.

BEGIN   **BEGIN <TEXT>**
Marks the start of a BEGIN-UNTIL or a BEGIN-WHILE-REPEAT loop. Some implementations also feature a BEGIN-AGAIN loop. Must be used in a colon definition.

BLK   **BLK addr**
Leaves the address of a variable that contains the mass storage block currently serving as the input stream on the stack.

BLOCK   **n BLOCK addr**
Leaves the address of the first byte in the block number specified. If the block is not yet in memory, it is transferred into a memory buffer.

BUFFER   **n BUFFER addr**
Assigns the next available memory buffer to the block number specified, but does not transfer the block from disk to memory.

C!   **n addr C!**
Stores the least significant 8 bits of the number specified at the address specified.

C@   **addr C@ byte**
Leaves the byte stored at the address specified on the stack. Since the stack is 16 bits wide, the most significant 8 bits are filled with zeros during the C@ operation.

CMOVE   **addr1 addr2 n CMOVE**
Moves the number of bytes specified from locations starting at the first address to new locations starting at the second address. The contents of memory are moved sequentially; thus, overlapping address requests may result in incomplete moves.

COMPILE   **COMPILE**

When a word containing COMPILE executes, the 16-bit number following the compilation address of COMPILE is copied into the dictionary. Thus, COMPILE CMOVE will copy the compilation address of CMOVE.

CONSTANT   **N CONSTANT <NAME>**

Defines a constant with the value and name specified. Afterward, whenever the name is executed, the value will be left on the stack.

CONTEXT   **CONTEXT addr**

Leaves the address of the variable that specified the vocabulary in which the dictionary searches for matching words.

CONVERT   **dl addr1 CONVERT d2 addr2**

Converts the text beginning at the first address to the second double number, which is left on the stack. The first double number is used as an accumulator, while the second address is the memory location of the first nonconvertible character.

COUNT   **addr COUNT addr+1 n**

Leaves the address plus 1 on the stack along with the character count of the text beginning at address+1.

CR   **CR**

Displays a carriage return and line feed on the current console device.

CREATE   **CREATE <NAME>**

Creates a dictionary entry without placing anything in the parameter field for the entry. When <NAME> is later executed, the address of the parameter field associated with that word is left on the stack.

CURRENT   **CURRENT addr**

Leaves the address of the variable that specifies the vocabulary into which new word definitions are being added.

D+   **d1 d2 D+ d3**

Adds two double numbers together.

D<   **d1 d2 D< flag**

Leaves a "true" value if the first double number is less than the second — otherwise "false."

DECIMAL   **DECIMAL**

Changes the current base to decimal.

DEFINITIONS   **DEFINITIONS**

Sets the variable CURRENT to the CONTEXT vocabulary. All new definitions are then created in the vocabulary selected by CONTEXT.

DEPTH   **DEPTH n**

Tells how many elements were on the stack before the word DEPTH executed.

DNEGATE   **d1 DNEGATE -d1**

Leaves the two's complement of a double number on the stack.

DO   **n1 n2 DO <TEXT>**

Begins an indexed loop that begins counting at the second number and is terminated when the index value would be equal to the first number. Must be used in colon definition.

DOES>   **: <NAME> CREATE <TEXT> DOES> ;**

Marks the termination of the defining portion of a CREATE sequence. (FIG-FORTH uses <BUILDS instead of CREATE.)

DROP   **n DROP**

Drops the top number from the stack.

DUP   **n DUP n n**

Duplicates the top number on the stack.

ELSE   **IF <TEXT1> ELSE <TEXT2> THEN**

Used to force conditional execution of <TEXT2> when entry into the IF function is "false." Must be used in a colon definition.

EMIT   **char EMIT**

Transfers the character to the current output device.

EMPTY-BUFFERS   **EMPTY-BUFFERS**

Marks all buffers as being empty and ready for reuse. Nothing is changed within the buffer, although blocks that have been marked by UPDATE are not written back to disk.

EXECUTE   **addr EXECUTE**

Executes the dictionary entry whose address is on the stack.

EXIT   **EXIT**

Used within a colon definition to terminate execution of that definition. May not be used within a DO loop.

EXPECT   **addr n EXPECT**

Transfers characters from the console to memory beginning at the address specified until a carriage return or the number of characters specified has been received.

FILL   **addr n byte FILL**

Fills number of bytes of memory beginning at address with the byte specified.

FIND   **FIND <NAME> addr**

Leaves the address of the next word on the stack.

FORGET   **FORGET <NAME>**

Causes the <NAME> to be deleted from the dictionary, as well as all words added to the dictionary after <NAME>.

FORTH   **FORTH**

FORTH is the name of the primary vocabulary.

HERE   **HERE addr**

Leaves the address of the next available dictionary location on the stack.

HOLD   **char HOLD**

Inserts the character specified into a pictured numeric ouptput sequence. May be used only between <# and #>.

I   **I n**

Leaves the loop index value of the outermost loop on the stack. May be used only within a DO loop.

IF   **flag IF <TYPE1> ELSE <TYPE2> THEN**

If "true," <TYPE1> executes; if "false," <TYPE2> executes. "ELSE <TYPE2>" may be omitted if the desired execution is execution only on true.

IMMEDIATE   **IMMEDIATE**

Marks the most recently made dictionary entry as a word that is executed within colon definitions rather than compiled.

J   **J n**

Leaves the loop-index value of the next-to-outermost loop on the stack. May be used only within an embedded DO loop.

KEY   **KEY char**

Leaves the ASCII value of the character available from the current input device.

LEAVE   **LEAVE**

Forces an early exit from a DO loop by setting the loop limit equal to the current value of the index.

LIST   **n LIST**

Displays in ASCII the contents of the numbered screen and changes the variable SCR to contain the number specified.

LITERAL   **n LITERAL**

Compiles the specified value into a definition, so that when the word defined later executes, the value is left on the stack.

LOAD   **n LOAD**

Begins input from the block number specified. Each character encountered while loading information from the block specified will be interpreted in the same manner as if it were being typed at the console.

LOOP

Terminates a DO loop which increments by 1.

MAX   **n1 n2 MAX n3**

Leaves the greater of two numbers on the stack.

MIN   **n1 n2 MIN n3**

Leaves the lesser of two numbers on the stack.

MOD   **n1 n2 MOD n3**

Divides n1 by n2, and leaves the remainder on the stack with the same sign as held by n1.

MOVE   **addr1 addr2 n MOVE**

Moves the specified number of 16-bit memory elements from memory beginning at the first address to memory beginning at the second address.

NEGATE   **n NEGATE -n**

Leaves the two's complement of a number (0 minus the number) on the stack.

NOT   **flag1 NOT flag2**

Reverses the value of the flag on the stack. Identical in operation to 0 =.

OR   **n1 n2 OR n3**

Performs a bit-wise inclusive-OR of the two numbers specified and leaves the result on the stack.

OVER   **n1 n2 OVER n1 n2 n1**

Duplicates the second element on the stack, in effect, making it both the first and third element on the stack.

PAD   **PAD addr**

Leaves the address of a 64-byte scratch pad area on the stack. Often used to "buffer" user input before processing.

PICK   **n1 PICK n2**

Duplicates the contents of the n1-th stack value (not counting n1, itself) and leaves it as the top element on the stack.

QUERY   **QUERY**

Accepts up to 80 characters (or all characters up to a carriage return if less than 80) and places them into a terminal input buffer. WORD can then be used to pick off characters from this buffer.

QUIT   **QUIT**

Clears the return stack, sets FORTH to the execution mode, and returns control to the user console. No message is given (that is, no "OK" is displayed).

R>   **R> n**

Transfers a value from the return stack to the data

R@   **R@ n**

Copies the number on the top of the return stack to the data stack.

REPEAT

Used within a colon-definition which contains a BEGIN-REPEAT loop.

ROLL   **n ROLL**

Moves the n-th element on the stack to the top position and adjusts the remaining elements accordingly.

ROT   **n1 n2 n3 ROT n2 n3 n1**

Rotates the top three elements on the stack so that the bottom-most becomes the new top element with the others moved down one position.

SAVE-BUFFERS **SAFE-BUFFERS**

Causes all blocks which have been flagged using UPDATE to be written to the appropriate location on the mass-storage device.

SCR **SCR addr**

Leaves the address of the variable which contains the screen most recently used (that is, the screen that was most recently listed or fetched).

SIGN **n SIGN**

Inserts the ASCII code for "-" (minus sign/hyphen) into the pictured numeric output string, if the number specified is negative.

SPACE **SPACE**

Transmits an ASCII "blank" to the current console

SPACES **n SPACES**

Transmits the specified number of ASCII "blanks" to the current console device.

STATE **STATE addr**

Leaves the address of the variable which contains the compilation state on the stack.

SWAP **n1 n2 SWAP n2 n1**

Exchanges the top two elements on the stack.

THEN

Used within a colon definition to terminate an IF statement.

TYPE **addr n TYPE**

Transmits the number of characters specified, from memory beginning at the address specified, to the console display.

U* **un1 un2 U* ud3**

Multiplies two unsigned numbers and leaves the result as an unsigned double number on the stack.

U. **un U.**

Displays the unsigned number specified in the current base on the console display, with one trailing blank following the free-formatted number.

U/MOD ud1 ud2 U/MOD un3 un4

Divides the first unsigned double number by the second and leaves the remainder and quotient as unsigned single numbers on the stack.

U< un1 un2 U< flag

Compares the two unsigned numbers and leaves a flag representing the "truth" of the statement "un1 < un2" on the stack.

UNTIL

Used within a colon definition to terminate a BEGIN loop.

UPDATE UPDATE

Marks the most recently referenced block as having been modified. Should the memory buffer the block occupies be needed for storage of another block, UPDATE tells FORTH that the memory buffer should be saved onto diskette.

VARIABLE VARIABLE <NAME>

Defines an entry for a variable with the name specified.

VOCABULARY VOCABULARY <NAME>

Defines an entry for an ordered list of word definitions. Used in conjunction with CURRENT and CONTEXT vocabulary.

WHILE

Used within a colon definition to termine a BEGIN loop.

WORD char WORD addr

Receives characters from the defined input stream until the delimited character specified is encountered or the input stream is exhausted.

[[

Ends the compilation mode and begins execution of text from the input stream.

[COMPILE [COMPILE] <NAME>

Used within a colon definition to force compilation of the named word. This allows for compilation of an IMMEDIATE word when it would otherwise be executed.

]]

Restarts the compilation mode and begins compiling all subsequent text from the input stream (see [, above).

Appendix C

ASCII Character Codes

Decimal Number	Coded Character	Decimal Number	Coded Character	Decimal Number	Coded Character	Decimal Number	Coded Character
0	^@	32	Space	64	@	96	`
1	^A	33	!	65	A	97	a
2	^B	34	"	66	B	98	b
3	^C	35	#	67	C	99	c
4	^D	36	$	68	D	100	d
5	^E	37	%	69	E	101	e
6	^F	38	&	70	F	102	f
7	^G	39	'	71	G	103	g
8	^H	40	(	72	H	104	h
9	^I	41	)	73	I	105	i
10	^J	42	*	74	J	106	j
11	^K	43	+	75	K	107	k
12	^L	44	'	76	L	108	l
13	^M	45	-	77	M	109	m
14	^N	46	.	78	N	110	n
15	^O	47	/	79	O	111	o
16	^P	48	0	80	P	112	p
17	^Q	49	1	81	Q	113	q
18	^R	50	2	82	R	114	r
19	^S	51	3	83	S	115	s
20	^T	52	4	84	T	116	t
21	^U	53	5	85	U	117	u
22	^V	54	6	86	V	118	v
23	^W	55	7	87	W	119	w
24	^X	56	8	88	X	120	x
25	^Y	57	9	89	Y	121	y
26	^Z	58	:	90	Z	122	z
27	Escape	59	;	91	[	123	{
28	FS	60	<	92	\	124		
29	GS	61	=	93	]	125	}
30	RS	62	>	94	^	126	~
31	US	63	?	95	<--	127	DEL

–Suggested Alternatives to the FORTH Syntax–

While FORTH fanatics might complain about this statement, there is nothing sacred about the names given to each word defined in FORTH. And, since you can easily change the names of words at any time, you might consider "personalizing" your version of FORTH.

The general format for redefining a word would be:

                    : NEWNAME OLDNAME ;

This results in a bit of additional overhead. Another possible method:

                    : NEWNAME
                        STATE @
                        IF
                            COMPILE OLDNAME
                        ELSE
                            OLDNAME
                        THEN ;
                        IMMEDIATE

Some suggested changes follow:

	FORTH		**COBOL Style**
change	!	to	STORE
	C!	to	STORE-BYTE
	@	to	FETCH
	C@	to	FETCH-BYTE
	.	to	DISPLAY
	."	to	DISPLAY-TEXT or just "
	;S	to	STOP-LOADING
	CMOVE	to	MOVE-BYTES
	MOD	to	MODULO
	SCR	to	SCREEN
	SP!	to	INIT-STACK
	SP@	to	FETCH-POINTER
	VLIST	to	LIST-WORDS
	ROT	to	ROTATE
	DUP	to	DUPLICATE
	CODE	to	ASSEMBLY
	END-CODE	to	END-ASSEMBLY

Again, these are only suggestions. There are pluses and minuses to changing the given names of FORTH words. If you think that such changes will help you learn FORTH more quickly, go ahead and make the changes. You can always change everything back later.

Error Messages

The error messages for most FORTH systems reside on block 0 and block 1 on the FORTH diskette. Since these blocks are changeable, just like any FORTH block, you may wish to change the messages to suit you. The error messages in FIG-FORTH look like the following:

ERROR NUMBER	MESSAGE
0	(ERROR MESSAGES)
1	EMPTY STACK
2	DICTIONARY FULL
3	HAS INCORRECT ADDRESS MODE
4	ISN'T UNIQUE
5	
6	DISC RANGE ?
7	FULL STACK
8	DISC ERROR !
9	
10	
11	
12	
13	
14	
15	FORTH INTEREST GROUP
16	(ERROR MESSAGES)
17	COMPILATION ONLY, USE IN DEFINITION
18	EXECUTION ONLY
19	CONDITIONALS NOT PAIRED
20	DEFINITION NOT FINISHED
21	IN PROTECTED DICTIONARY
22	USE ONLY WHEN LOADING
23	OFF CURRENT EDITING SCREEN
24	DECLARE VOCABULARY
25	
26	
27	
28	
29	
30	
31	

Most other versions of FORTH modify these slightly, leaving the same intent for each message, but wording the messages so that they are clearly comprehensible.

0	Mythical FORTH Version 1-1
1	The stack is empty.
2	The dictionary is full
3	has incorrect address mode.
4	isn't unique
5	An obscure error of the fifth kind has occurred.
6	Illegal block number requested.
7	The stack is full.
8	
9	
10	
11	
12	CP/M Error — Seek to unwritten extent.
13	CP/M Error — Directory overflow.
14	CP/M Error — Seek past physical end of disk.
15	
16	Second System Message Screen
17	is legal only within a colon definition.
18	is not legal within a colon definition.
19	The expression contains unpaired conditionals.
20	The definition has not been finished.
21	is within the protected dictionary.
22	should only be used while loading.
23	Off current editing screen.
24	Please declare a vocabulary.
25	The current file is closed. Please OPEN a file.
26	Binary Data — Cannot be displayed directly.
27	JanFebMarAprMayJunJulAugSepOctNovDecMonTueWedThuFriSatSun
28	
29	
30	
31	

NOTE: Since each error message takes up 64 characters whether you need that many or not, it doesn't make any sense to create cryptic or abbreviated messages (unless, of course, you like cryptic or abbreviated error messages).

Some FORTH Extensions

As explained in the main text of this book, FORTH is an extensible language. You may add any feature you think the language may be lacking. Two such extensions are shown below.

CASE Structure

The Pascal {CASE} statement is useful for directing program execution to one of several sections of code, dependent upon the value of a variable. In FORTH, the value of the top element on the stack will point to the section of code to be executed when the {CASE} function is executed.

```
4      (value on stack)
CASE
   1 OF do-first-thing  ENDOF
   2 OF do-second-thing ENDOF
   3 OF do-third-thing  ENDOF
   4 OF do-fourth-thing ENDOF
   do-otherwise-things
ENDCASE
```

In the above example, since "4" was the value upon execution of {CASE}, only FORTH {do-fourth-thing} would be executed. If the value had been "2," only {do-second-thing} would have been executed. If the value had not been "1," "2," "3," or "4," {do-otherwise-things} would have been executed.

Here's the coding needed to add {CASE}, {OF}, {ENDCASE}, and {ENDOF} to your version of FORTH. NOTE: The following code has only been tested using FIG-FORTH, but should work with most "standard" FORTHs.

```
:CASE        (Execute Code Based On Stack Value)

  ?COMP CSP @ !CSP 4 ;

IMMEDIATE

: OF

  4 ?PAIRS COMPILE

  OVER COMPILE

  = COMPILE
```

```
    0BRANCH HERE 0, COMPILE
    DROP 5 ;
IMMEDIATE
:ENDOF
  5 ?PAIRS COMPILE
  BRANCH HERE 0, SWAP 2
  [COMPILE THEN
  4 ;
IMMEDIATE
: ENDCASE
  4 ?PAIRS COMPILE
  DROP
  BEGIN
     SP@ CSP @ =
   0 = WHILE
     2 [COMPILE
   THEN
  REPEAT
  CSP ! ;
IMMEDIATE
```

FORTH words